The Humanitarian

A Novel

By N. Caraway

'But say a man does know. He sees the world as it is and he looks back thousands of years to see how it all came about. He sees how men have to rob their brothers in order to live and he sees children starving and women workings sixty hours a week to get to eat. He sees a whole damn army of unemployed and billions of dollars and thousands of miles wasted. He sees war coming. He sees how when people suffer just so much they get mean and ugly and something dies in them. But the main thing he sees is that the whole system of the world is built on a lie. And although it's as plain as the shining sun – the don't-knows have lived with that lie so long they just can't see it.'

**Carson McCullers, 'The heart is a lonely hunter'**

# Preface

I am no different from so many others, inhabitants all of us of a shrinking planet. Every few years I pack up all my belongings. The removal men come and carefully put away the things that will accompany me to some other sprawling city. They leave and I hang around for a day or two, half enjoying the ghostlike quality of my continued presence after the goodbye party has drawn a line under my existence in the minds of the workmates and colleagues with whom I have shared a brief and vivid interlude of meetings and coffee shops. They know that the promises to keep in touch, to send emails, meet up at headquarters - all these things that are, after all, made so easy these days – will not be kept. Time moves on and it seems the more we are able to extend our individual lifelines around the world, the more we live the lives we live in isolation.

Sometimes I can close my eyes and see those lines, like small tangled threads, wrapping the planet round and round like an untidy ball of string. Everyone has been everywhere, work, holidays, migration, retirement combined in a striving to fulfill that unappeasable urge we have inside to escape from real or imagined drudgery into the land beyond the rainbow's end. And when circumstances prevent us temporarily or permanently from boarding our ships and sailing the wine-dark sea, we watch television programmes that are skillfully designed to take our minds to the places our feet cannot reach.

My own life has not deviated much from this norm. In my case it has been work rather than the lure of travel brochures that has taken me from one distant capital to another, places I never seemed to chose and always viewed beforehand with a degree of trepidation that would inevitably subside into a mixture of mild disappointment and relief as the exotic imaginings conjured in my mind by memories of schoolboy history or hasty perusal of newspaper supplements gave way to the reality of another indifferent steel and concrete streetscape where familiar brands of clothing, coffee, fast food and hotel chains winked and throbbed their neon promise of the comforts of globalised English-speaking familiarity.

Departure is always followed by a period of uncertainty, a sense of not belonging anywhere that is accompanied by an inner excitement, a sensation of total freedom made poignant by an acute awareness of its transitory nature and the inevitable march of days and slow creep of life. It is a time when each morning begins with the conviction that the sun's rays will bring the life-changing event that is destined finally to give this individual existence the meaning it has been chasing all along. The days go by and the woman of my dreams fails to appear, the lottery ticket with the winning number is not bought, the letter from a mysterious unknown relative does not come. The new assignment begins to loom, heavy and oppressive like a storm on the horizon. Appointments are made for medical examinations, visas, briefings. I do some shopping, send messages to old friends in the hope that they will reply one day, visit favourite places in the town where I grew up and to which I inevitably return at the end of each assignment, drawn like a homing pigeon, even though there is no family or friend waiting for me there. And then I leave. It would have been no different this last time. I had left Dhaka, left the rickshaws and the smell and the perpetuum mobile of the straggling lines of garment factory girls shuffling between the boshtis where they live and the sweatshops where they work. I was staying in my usual bed and breakfast near the river, across which I could see the green expanse of parkland through which my customary path would lead me towards the towers and spires of the ancient university-dominated town centre. My spirits were still high with the gypsy sense of detachment from all that was regular and fixed. I was free for a while to come and go as I pleased, to rise late and stroll over to my favourite café, where I could read the newspapers while consuming a 'full English breakfast'. This was something I would only do during these 'in-between' times. Like everyone else, I know that fatty foods, like bacon, and the high cholesterol of egg yokes, are bad for the health, but this does not matter when I am between postings, because at such times I am a ghost and nothing I consume can affect me. I will regularise my diet, like every other aspect of my life, once I have settled into the new place.

And so I was on the point of leaving my bedroom when a ray of early morning sunlight drew my attention to the pile of what I had taken to be old magazines left by the landlady on the small table by the window. I looked at them for a moment or two from across the room, aware that there was something different about them but, deprived as yet of the caffeine I need in order to deal effectively with the start of the day, unable to determine what it was. Then I went over and picked the top one up, seeing at once that it was not a magazine at all but an old school exercise book. When I opened it I found hand-written text. A place name and a date and then, in an untidy scribbled hand, the beginning of a journal. I quickly thumbed through the other documents. They were a mixture of hardback notebooks, writing pads of the cheap variety you can get at any stationers and school exercise books with the name of a school that did not include its location. They were all full of the same untidy scribbling in a variety of colours of ink. Some of the pages were torn and others were stained with red earth and brown coffee. Others began with school exercises written in a different hand altogether, presumably that of the child for whom the exercise book had originally been intended. Time was passing and I was hungry and desperate for coffee. I took the top book with me and set off to get my breakfast.

After I had eaten my eggs and bacon and was onto my second cup of coffee, a point at which I would normally have turned to the morning's edition of The Independent or The Guardian, or possibly even the Times, I opened the exercise book and started to read the story that Richards had set out in his messy script and I found myself observing him quite clearly in my mind, in a detached manner, but with an undeniable, increasing degree of engagement, as he squatted or lay alone in his tent in the middle of a vast, empty country that I knew I would never see. I found myself wondering what had driven him to write and who on earth he thought he was writing for. And I wondered, more mundanely, what aberration had caused him to leave his manuscript in my bedroom.

I had been planning to spend the morning wandering around my favourite bookshops, but an unexpected restlessness now had me in its grip. Richards had been unhappy and lonely and his mood was disturbing my equilibrium. I wanted to rid myself of him. I went back to the bed and breakfast and rang the landlady's bell with the intention of giving the manuscript to her so that she could return it to its owner, who must have been the previous occupant of the room. It took a long time for her to come to her door and when she got there she had the irritated look that landladies and landlords have on their faces during the hours when guests are not supposed to disturb them. She listened to me with pursed lips and eventually interrupted before I could finish making the suggestion that I bring the notebooks down to her. 'Oh no,' she said. 'That won't do. Those papers have been there for at least two years now. I've no idea whose they are. They'll have to stay where they are. I can't throw them away in case whoever it was that left them comes back for them... Unless you want to take them with you and see if you can do something?'

She added this last suggestion after an almost imperceptible pause, as though it was not an altogether spontaneous remark.

No doubt, I told myself, she would have been very pleased to be rid of the encumbrance of these messy bits and pieces which her conscience would not allow her to consign to the dustbin. Her ever so slightly hopeful tone of voice made me determined that I definitely would not oblige her by taking the papers with me. I did not want to fill my mind with the lonely misery of some other lost globe-trotter at precisely the moment when I was about to plunge into the stressful business of establishing myself once again in a new and distant country. So I left the notebooks where they were and went back into town.

After a disappointing morning meandering around the piles of outsize semi-paperbacks with lurid, covers and improbable names that purport to be literature these days, reminding myself once more that the bookshops I wanted to revisit had changed so much that they no longer resembled the quiet, slightly academic refuges of cherished memory, I came back to pack my bags and, possibly without thinking but quite probably also with a degree of unfinalised volition, I included Richards' diary in all its messy exercise and note books with my things.

I did not look at it again for many weeks, not until long after I had settled into my comfortable if rather characterless apartment in the business district of Manila. Then I started to read, a small amount each evening, and as I did so, the realisation crept over me that this might have been my own life, but in a different place with different people. Little by little a restlessness began to infect me as this idea took hold of my imagination. Richards' journal became my own possession, although I did not fall into the delusion that I had in any sense created it. I had never wanted to be a writer. Reading had always been enough for me. But Richards' journal needed to be worked on and almost inevitably I started to tidy it up, transforming the scribbled entries he must have made by torchlight in his muddy tent into something more literary, I suppose, if by that what I mean is the organisation of text into chapters and some editing to remove mistakes and repetitions.

I happened to be reading a battered old penguin edition of a novel by a long forgotten American novelist, one that I had found in the open bookshelves outside the second hand bookshop that still remains relatively unchanged in its secluded location in a narrow pedestrian passage in the very centre of my hallowed old home town and to which I had hurried to seek refuge from the stifling, claustrophobia of the shopping malls that had oppressed my soul to a point where it seemed to suck the life out of veins . Some words there seemed to match the desperate mood that characterized Richards' lonely scribbles, so I copied them out and inserted them as an opening quotation. The effect was pleasing and gave me an undue sense of my own creativity, as if I had composed them, rather than simply copying them out.

Then, some weeks later, one hot and humid tropical morning as I sprawled on the day bed I had established on the covered veranda, or lanay as they called it, that ranged along one side of my house in one of manicured gated villages where the rich and the expatriate communities of Manila are domiciled, thumbing through the last remaining notebook in a clumsy, torpid manner as the galvinising effect of my breakfast coffee began to wear off, a stained and slightly torn photograph dropped out of it onto the ground at my feet. I bent down slowly in order to guard against any sudden rush of blood to the head, picked it up and found myself looking at a lean, sad looking man in a sunhat surrounded by naked children, somewhere in Africa. And I knew immediately, with that peculiar combination of certainty and breathless shock that comes with suddenly bumping into a long-lost friend, that I was looking at him.

I wonder sometimes what he would have thought of the end product of my unsolicited collaboration, if he could have seen it wherever it may be that he has ended up. If he came to claim it, whose text in the end would it actually be? The notebooks are his and I have done my very best to maintain and conserve the restless urgency of his unhappy voice. But the story I have set out here has cost me a lot of work. I have extracted the essence of the man and inserted it into the lonely terror of his last desperate journey into the emptiness that he thought was outside in the endless swamps and savannah, but which was all the time lurking and smirking within.

Looking back over this endeavour, I have to say that a lot of myself, not just my hard work, but something from inside me, something of who I am, has gone into this labour, even if it has not been – and I must insist on this - a labour of love.

# I.

*Thursday night*

*It is Thursday night. I repeat this information several times over to myself. It is Thursday the eighteenth of September 2003. The date is a hard, concrete element in the swaying flux that has swallowed me up and made me disappear. I can hold onto it, like a shipwrecked sailor holding onto a lifeline, or like Theseus in the labyrinth holding onto the thread that will guide him out, a thread that started in Nairobi and led through Loki and then out here into the darkness beyond. When the job is done I am going to haul myself back in on this lifeline. Back to Loki. In the meantime I am out here, past the point where firm and rational things end, out in the timeless place without form or boundaries. The date is what lets me measure the distance along the line I have come and what I still have left to go. Holding onto the line gives me comfort and keeps that little spark of hope or courage or whatever it is alive that will get me through.*

I switched on the small electric torch and felt for my wrist watch on the canvas floor of the tent next to the camp bed. Just eight p.m. The night had hardly begun, but already the thick cloud of mosquitoes had driven me into this cramped, sealed-in tomb.

My arms and forehead were sore from sunburn. There had been no vehicles and we had had to walk to every destination we needed to cover in the survey. The Sudanese glided through the grassland without water or provisions, smooth, calm and fast, and I had been stretched to stay up with them, almost trotting, like a child among adults. Now my lower back was throbbing with a nagging pain from ligaments torn long before in a different place and a different life.

All the time we had been walking I could sense that they were testing me, or mocking me perhaps, pleased to see me suffer for the way I had pushed so hard and insistently for us to go to places that they could just have told me about. They could so easily have given numbers and figures and tales of failed harvest and dead cattle. That would have been sufficient for the report that would one day bring the big plane and the food drop. Only a 'faranji', an outsider from Nairobi, would insist on doing things the hard way, so in return they were going to let me have it hard. That had been the essence of their thought and it had seemed as I walked, with my mind drunk and drifting in the heat haze, that I could reach out and touch it in the shimmering air above the head-high grass through which we trekked past red termite hills and acacia trees that tantalised with the offer of shade too far from the path to be of any use.

Further north the rains had come already and the grasslands they call the 'toic' had already made their annual transformation into the world's largest swamp. I would have been better off down there under the dense cloud cover, soaked to the skin, cold and up to my waste in water at times, or crouched in a narrow canoe. My water bottle had run dry and I had started to dehydrate. By the time we got back to our camp my urine had become so concentrated that it came out in a steaming, dark brown river that burned my innards like a fire as it passed, leaving a residual pain that kept me awake and restless now.

I reached up and touched the canvas roof of the tent that was too close above my head. Then I turned the torch off. The batteries were running low, not only in the torch, but in the little shortwave radio that let me tune into the BBC early in the morning when the transmission sometimes got through and also in the Thuraya sat phone that was my only link to the real world that still existed outside all of this, back up the line.

Apart, that was, from the obligatory early morning radio call to Loki on the long wave radio we had set up on arrival. But then that did not really count. A few moments of coded jargon did not make you feel part of anything.

It was not as though there was anyone in particular to phone back there, but it was good to know I could and, when it came, the thought that sudden rain swamping the airstrip could trap me here for an extra week took my spirits down in a sudden deep dive that came close to panic. In that time we would run out of safe food, clean water and batteries. If it rained, getting out on time would all depend on whether on the scheduled flight day the WFP controller chose to send a Caravan or a Twin Otter. A Twin Otter would probably be able to land, but a Caravan wouldn't. I hoped it would not rain, despite the huge thunderheads that built up in the northern skies each day. And I hoped the plane would be a Twin Otter when it came. For now, though, there was still the best part of a week to go. Today was Thursday and we were due out on the following Tuesday. That made five days.

I lay in the darkness, shifting from side to side, trying to ease the burning pain in my lower abdomen. I could hear the voices of my Sudanese colleagues. They were sitting round the fire, oblivious to the mosquitoes, talking and laughing in Juba Arabic. I guessed they were discussing politics, the old Sudan and the new. It was all they every talked about, the only topic of interest. The whole grisly twenty year old conflict was just a big game, a cattle raid, a gamble, the way life was and had been and would be. The Southern leaders had been part of the government in the past and soon they would be part of it again, in spite of all the talk of independence, and they seemed happy with the game, the uncertainty of a politics that reflected the old, unchanging ways of doing things, the politics of transhumance. It was not quite that simple, of course. There were other factors, the resources for one thing, especially the oil which the Chinks were busy grabbing. That was what was causing all the shit these days….

I rolled on my side, but the pain would not go away and sleep would not come. When I closed my eyes I saw the woman and the child standing just inside the gateway to passport control, past that point where I could still touch them. The child was waving and saying something: 'Look after my toys'. His voice was serious. The woman smiled at this and hugged the child: 'Say goodbye to Daddy.' Then I turned and walked away before they did. And that had been the last time I saw them. How long ago now? I could still remember the exaggerated clarity of her foreigner English, a good copy of the educated Scots accent of the teacher she had had when she first came to London.

Now there was no-one. No-one to talk to on the Thuraya that lay on the ground next to my head, like a chunky, oversized cell-phone. I stopped myself from going down the line of thinking that was opening up. I hated myself for the self-pity when it started to show. At least no-one else ever got to see it or know about it. It had all been a long time ago, in any case, and I was used to being alone. I told myself I preferred it, in fact. That was why I had taken this assignment, the logical endpoint of a progression, sometimes deliberate and sometimes, on the surface at least, accidental, further and further away from the places where people dressed up in suits and said 'Good Morning' to each other and communicated or 'interacted', as they say, by email and fax and phone and word and smile.

Loud laughter from over by the fire pulled me out of my inner world for a second and I lay listening. John the trainee evangelical preacher was saying something and the others were laughing. I wondered what it was. My Arabic was not quite good enough ever to pick up on their own peculiar variant of it and they would always switch to English when they wanted to communicate with me, which was not usually in the evening after eating.

Then they fell silent and after a few moments I heard them sorting out their tents, clearing their throats and spitting and cleaning their teeth in preparation for turning in. I could hear something else now, too: drumbeats coming from the village, soft and muffled in the night, and the snorting and bellowing of the cattle, corralled for the night somewhere near the centre of the village. The young boys would have herded them down at dusk from their grazing halfway up the hillside, driving them with long sticks to keep them moving, fast and reckless. The only other sounds were the endless screech of the insects and the burping of frogs. There was no electricity here – no electricity, no roads, no safe water for several hundred miles. To the northwest the grasslands sloped gently down into the Nile swamps, to the South they dried away into the badlands and deserts of the Kenya border and to the east the hills rose abruptly towards Ethiopia. This place was a nowhere place, just a meeting point of different terrains and peoples; its name simply meant 'Campsite', the site of the first base the SPLA had set up when they moved in from Ethiopia all those years before. They still had a big garrison sitting on the escarpment above the village, ready to fight and ready to run back across the border if need be.

It was hot in the tent and a rank smell came from the pile of sweaty clothes that lay in the corner, fusing with the stale odour of the canvas and the acrid stink of the mud in the yard outside and underneath my body below the thin ground sheet. If it rained the whole place would turn into a gooey, stinking cesspit. I had left the outer flap open with just the mosquito netting inner sheet zipped up in the hope of catching any whisper of a breeze, but the air was still. I lay on my back again now, feeling the sweat begin to form a puddle on my chest. I was wearing a thin t-shirt and the old kikoy I always used at night. The kikoy felt like too much material around my overheated limbs. I pulled it away from my legs and groin and threw it down onto the floor of the tent. A scuttling noise erupted behind the small pile of books and equipment, the things I always travelled with, my comfort things - the second hand Evans Pritchard, the star book, the knot-tying book, the guide to radio codes, the first aid manual, the maps, the poorly printed SRRC code of conduct and rule book, my passport, the SRRC pass, the survival kit with the guinea worm filter, the lighter, luminescent stick, fish hooks, compass, foil security blanket, Chinese malaria medicine, antiseptic spray and bandages. I used to look at those things and tell myself I would always be at home in the bush. If anything happened, I would walk out on my own. I would find something better than people if that ever happened and I would come through cured and calm. These precious things took up a lot of space in my small pack, but they all mattered.

Then I heard the noise again.

There wasn't a lot of room in the tent and I did not want to get too close to whatever was making the noise. I eased myself down to a kneeling position next to the camp bed, fumbled for the torch and switched it on. I shone the small beam towards the books and carefully reached out and moved them one by one onto the bed. There was nothing behind them. I started to move the other stuff, too, piece by piece onto the bed. I was half way down the pile when something darted behind the heap of dirty clothes in the corner. It was fast, but I saw it well, a large flat spider, the sort you usually got on the walls of the huts. I was pretty sure they were harmless, but it filled me with fear, the fear of a child for nightmares and darkness, nothing rational or sane. I knew I could rest while it was still in the tent with me. I put the torch down on the camp bed so that the beam pointed towards the pile of clothes. Then I began to move them one by one, lifting each item careful and shaking it hard before depositing it on top of the other things on the bed. Halfway through the spider dropped suddenly from the sweat-soaked underpants I had worn that day. I brought the shoe down hard on it just as it landed and then ground it savagely, working it round and round, grinding down as hard as I could, feeling my teeth clench until the tension dissolved as the frenzy of fear and anger spent itself.

When I lifted the shoe all I could see underneath was a curled-up, shapeless lump of slightly sticky muck on the floor of the tent. By morning the tiny ants that nothing could keep out would have dealt with it and the tent would be clean again.

It was too early to be lying here. The fear of using up my remaining battery power kept me from reading. Evans Pritchard had not turned out to be good bed-time reading in any case. His style was too dry and scientific. I wondered what sort of a man he had been, camping alone in his tent deep in the Nuer heartlands, taking his time, the way they always seemed to do in those days ever since the times of Burton and Baker. Months would go by and they would not seem concerned. Nowadays a day could seem like an age. Maybe the close familiarity of easy communication had changed the way people perceived time and the way they coped with the big empty spaces. First there were telephones and fax and now mobile phones and email. You were not supposed to get yourself into a situation where none of that worked anymore; nobody did that.

It was always best, though, to try to be dry and factual. That was what kept you able to cope when the nights closed in one after another and the day brought no relief, only burning heat. I tried breathing slowly, the way I had learned from the Indian yoga teacher in Nairobi. Then I started to run the trip through my mind sequentially, like a film in the cutting room.

I was here to participate in the Annual Needs Assessment. They did it every year to determine how much imported grain and other foodstuffs they were going to distribute. They always waited for the onset of the rainy season, as though the whole point was to make it difficult and uncomfortable to carry out. Someone had once said that it was just the way their planning cycle went - the weather was just an irrelevant inconvenience. At the end of the day the figures would be arbitrary enough and would result in a food aid distribution that would be a more-or-less standard one third smaller that what was distributed in the north – that was dictated by the politics of appeasing the government in Khartoum.

I had flown in with two other team members, both Southern Sudanese. One of them, John, was an SPLA veteran of the 1982 battle of Torit, now working for WFP, but also training to be a preacher with an African evangelical church of some sort, the other, Samuel, was a nutritionist working for one of the NGOs affiliated to Operation Lifeline Sudan. John was a typical Dinka to look at, tall and lean. Samuel was shorter and overweight, though he was also a Dinka. They started every meeting and every meal with a long prayer.

They had to fill in a complicated household food economy form. The Sudanese had been on a WFP training course, but it didn't seem to have done much for them. They seemed very unsure of themselves. The team leader had failed to show up in Loki and now they were out on their own and my presence seemed to inhibit them. On the first day we had sat in the compound outside the tents talking with the local chiefs to try and get some gauge on the situation. The whole business was flawed. Anyone could have seen that from the first handshake with the local SRRC chief. His name was Simon. He smiled a lot and tried to make sure that he did all the talking. It was his way of staying in charge. The first thing he said was to explain that he was in charge - in charge of the village, of the distribution of aid and of everything we were going to do. He explained how he had been the RAS representative before the unification with the SRRA, which gave birth do the SRRC. Now he was the SRRC administrator and his power had been doubled. He was wearing a scuffed and battered pair of black shoes, which set him apart from the rest of the community. They mostly went bare food or else used plastic flip-flops.

Simon had got the elders together under the mango tree and then had done all the translating. The people were Murle. The first thing you could see when you met them was that they had fewer of their lower teeth knocked out than the Dinka or Nuer. Other than that they were similar in build – tall, loose-limbed and thin. Evans Pritchard said they used to be feared for their ability to steal into Nuer villages in the night and kidnap children. I had always been fascinated by the thought of that. If even the Nuer feared them, then they must have something special. I had tried to find out more. Then in Nairobi I had once met an old retired missionary, who took away all the magic and the mystery, explaining that in fact endemic venereal disease had all but destroyed their own ability to procreate, so adopting or 'stealing' children from the Nuer had became essential for their survival.

Meeting them now in the flesh, far from the exotic darkness of anthropological tourism, these old people were something of a let down. They belched freely as they talked and both men and women broke off from speaking every now and then to spit dark stained saliva in long ribbons across the yard. Samuel tried out the participatory appraisal techniques with shiny lulu beans which he tipped gently out of a small cloth bag as though they were diamonds onto a chart. He looked self-conscious, almost guilty, like a fraudster caught in the act. The old people came forward quickly to pile the beans into little piles. They had done this too often before and they knew what it was about. The piles would accumulate according to whatever they had decided they wanted in the next big hand-out from the sky. Everybody knew the game, everybody played it out here. Only I was the new-comer this time, the uninvited guest from where they made the rules and where they would make the decisions, come to see that everybody played fair.

Simon sat behind on his battered wooden chair, smiling too much and translating the questions and the answers. There was no way to tell if what he told us was what the old people were really saying, no way to tell whether the first sorghum crop of the year really had failed, no way to know if it was true that most of the cattle were dead.

We had noted down all the answers because that was what we had to do. Somehow we had to fill in all the questions on crop types, yields, other sources of livelihood month by month across the year. We needed to get it all – livelihoods, nutrition, crop survey, somehow combining what the SRRC and the people it chose to present were saying with the evidence of their eyes. The numbers were totalled at the bottom and a formula converted it into quantities of grain, oil and other things to be delivered.

It had been clear from that first afternoon that it would not work. My colleagues were unsure of themselves. The training course had not prepared them for this and Simon could sit and keep his gate, smiling all the time. The information was his to give and his to create. I had seen the smile that twinkled in Simon's eyes before, the smile of the new elite, waiting to have its day. The other two knew it too and it did not bother them. Why should it? In the end goods would be delivered and the SPLM would take control one way or the other. Their conversation round the fire that first evening had confirmed it, as they waited for the women to cook the potatoes and cabbage they had brought with them from Loki.

There was no other food apart from what we had brought with us, though. In the small market old women sold Ethiopian cigarettes and Ethiopian tea, but nothing else.

I had listened to them saying that they might as well just sit under the mango tree each day and let Simon bring people to them from the surrounding area and it had irritated me, the way complacency always did. I did not want to be fat and slow and stupid, taken for a ride by the laughing Simon. If the team leader had been an experienced person well versed in the wiles of the myriad Simons spread across the wide sprawl of South Sudan, teamed up with an agronomist and a real, thorough-going nutritionist, then they'd get the data they needed without paying too much attention to the numbers they were told, they would see and count and measure, deduce and infer.

I had said as much to the others once Simon had gone, leaving us to eat our stewed vegetables in the dark. I had opened one of the tins of tuna I had brought for emergencies and shared it with them. That had brought us closer together for a while, as I had meant it to, so that I could talk openly with them in the spirit of hospitality and comradeship. I had said that we should get out and about as much as we could, in spite of Simon's advice that this would be futile, maybe because of it. And they had agreed, smiling in the fire glow, but silently making it clear that it was up to me to take the lead and to take responsibility for forcing the issue, leading them to wherever they would go and taking the blame if it all went wrong or nothing worthwhile came of it.

By day two the exasperation had been enough to give me the energy and resolution to wake them all early, shouting through the canvas walls of the tents in a harsh white man's voice. I had been too nervous and too full of early morning bad temper to disguise the lack of warmth in its tone. I had been up since dawn. I had cleaned my teeth while the frogs were still croaking and the laughing doves cooed in the trees of the compound, their call a liquid bubbling that tailed off like a spun coin vibrating to a stop on a wooden table top. I had waited with growing impatience as the sun's rays came over the hills in the east and I had packed my kit, checked it again and repacked it. Then my impatience had boiled over, just as the church drums were starting up in a deep, rhythmic throb from somewhere in the centre of the village and the high pitched unison singing of the children rose to mask my own angry ranting.

Of course I had been stupid to think I would get things my way. The others took their time performing their ablutions. The village women assigned to look after the visitors appeared silently from behind the SRRC office at the far end of the compound and began slowly cleaning the cooking pots left out after dinner and re-kindled the fire. John eventually came over to the gate to tell me tea was ready. Simon would not be there to join us until nine o'clock, he told me, and the SRRC would not permit us to go without him. They had known that the evening before, but had chosen not to tell me. In any case, they still had to do the radio check with Loki and give the weather report.

The sun was already high and hot when we had set off.

That first walk had been ten miles each way without shade. The effortless way the Sudanese seemed to glide through the bush, unaffected by heat or thirst, while I struggled just to keep up, made me curse them in my mind for not keeping to my plan of setting out in the cool darkness before dawn. The halfway point was marked by a single massive inselberg that reared up like a huge anthill out of the bush. Its jagged outline shimmered in the hot air as we trekked towards it, never seeming to grow any closer, perpetually vague and just out of reach until we passed it well over to the side and it just melted away leaving only the big wide horizon ahead.

On the way we had talked about the customs of the Murle. Simon told us about the November festival on the Lekongole river. It started with a dance, he said. Everybody had to dance making as much noise as possible on both banks to scare away all the crocodiles. Then they sacrificed goats, throwing the bodies into the river for the reptiles to seize and rip in the red stained waters. And then there was sex. Lots and lots of sex, an orgy without rules. That was the main point of it all. It was the one time when the rules did not allow a man to revenge himself on another man who slept with his wife. Simon smiled with a look of extreme lechery on his face and licked his lips as he said this and John and Samuel both laughed. It sounded like the way things might have been in the early days of the Greeks, a yearly ritual to renew the gene pool or purge the dark, Dionysian urges. I had caught myself starting to theorise and then had caught the glint in Simon's eye and had started to wonder if the whole story was not just a great big fabrication invented to make a fool of the bad-tempered white guy. In the heat their laughter became a nightmare.

The approach to the village had been marked by a treeless zone – everything close to the village must have become firewood long before – and a small herd of cattle. The village had been the usual messy straggle of huts with outdoor hearths for cooking and naked children playing amongst the ashes and the chickens. A group of villagers had sat down dutifully with the visitors in a circle on the ground and politely played with the lulu beans.
I had wanted something more than this, something to justify the long march. I told Samuel the nutritionist that he ought to have a proper look around to check the smallest children and babies for sighs of disease or malnutrition. Why had he not

been doing this from the moment of our arrival in any case? I could not understand this lack of enthusiasm or lack of initiative. Or was it a lack of self-confidence? When you came to face it, the two Sudanese had been in the field for so long, both of them, that it seemed to drain them of any initiative or desire. Its vast indifference had engulfed every last drop of enterprise long ago.

In the end I had to concede that the village had no special story to tell us beyond the poverty that twenty years of conflict had turned into the status quo. The lulu beans had nothing to say beyond the unsurprising fact that food aid was now an important part of the household economy.

Halfway through the afternoon we had got back and I had collapsed in my tent after two cups of tea made tasty with the spices I had brought with me as a little, comfort-giving luxury. Then for the first time I had passed urine the colour of coffee that burnt my urethra so badly that an hour later the pain still had me writing on my camp bed. I had risen again and gone to take a sweaty shit in the evil-smelling, fly-infested long-drop, before showering with the bucket.

I rolled onto my back again, staring into the darkness. A slight gust caused the tied back tent flap to rustle and I felt a cool air-stream blowing onto my legs. I shivered and pulled the kikoy back up off the floor and spread it like a blanket over my lower body and legs. The shivering continued and I wondered if this was sunstroke or the onset of malaria. It was most likely the former. I had taken so much direct sunlight during the last few days.

I wanted to sleep, to stop thinking and let my body and mind refresh themselves in preparation for the next day's challenge. The plan was to climb the hill that rose abruptly beyond the compound, dividing the community into two, to visit the communities who lived up above in the cooler, upland air - tribes whose territory extended to the border and beyond. I had promised my colleagues it would be the last big walk. After that we would spend the remaining days sitting at the table under the big fig tree in the SRRC compound, trying to make sense of the numbers and figures we had written down, mixing the spurious statistics supplied by Simon with the results of the participatory bean counts.

Tomorrow might be the best day yet, the day that would make up for all the disappointment so far. The tribes would be interesting. I had heard about them, Kachipo and Suri. Their women used lip plates, like the Mursi the tourists went to see down the Omo valley on the Ethiopian side. I knew that country, of course and in my mind I could sentimentalise the memories into something precious, lost and yet preserved.

But sleep would not come. The feeling of impotent, thwarted rage was there like a demon that sucked my strength, parasitically deep inside, waiting for these moments in the dark when I was alone and weak.

There were things that made me squirm, the memories of weakness and failure, the history I would go over again and again without a crumb of comfort, the impotence of the worm that can never turn. The summons to meet the Resident Coordinator in Khartoum had come at the end of a cross-line trip that hadn't worked. The Secretary General's special envoy had insisted on the trip, sensing a historic moment in the peace process and the chance for spurious glory. It would have been the first cross-line trip of its kind, calling at every destination that mattered, every enclave, both sides of the Nuba Mountains. That made it look good. And it had started well. We had got to see Garang in Rumbek. Paunchy and old in faded Bermudas, he had looked us up and down, the clean khakis and the elderly white faces, and gestured unsmilingly to the shade of a tree in a corner of the shabby compound, while he and his cronies conducted affairs of state in the leisurely manner of those who held real power in the grasslands, white haired and rich in cattle, slow and sure in their ways. When the court had been held and the chiefs rose, the visitors had been invited to sit down with them to eat the meal of goat's stomach and slimy okra stew that the women had prepared. And there was nothing for it but to sit and exchange meaningless pleasantries as the sun sank towards late afternoon and the pilot's deadline came and went. When we got back to the airstrip he had said it was too late to fly – for the first time from an SPLM-held location – to Juba, where the wali had been kept waiting in vain to meet the plane under the hot sun at the airstrip. The envoy had raged in vain. Everything was sabotage – by Garang, by the flight office, by WFP, by everyone.

The thing was that when these things happened and the self-appointed great and good lost their cool, it could never be a good thing to be around. In the end the shame they came to feel at their own impotence would condense into a hatred of those who witnessed it. Following a crazy UN logic of his own, the envoy had cancelled all the other stops, leaving the wali in Kadugali waiting under the sun just the same as the one in Juba, while, instead, a bumpy flight in a Caravan had taken the party in a straight line north into a full-blown haboob that filled the drab streets of El Obeid with angry orange dust. And from there we had flown in silence to Khartoum for the usual round of meetings with all the various government ministries and the mixture of embassies and aid agencies and missions that called itself the donor community. The envoy had not spoken another word to me, but I had seen his nakedness.

I had ended up hating the job and hating the UN. All I wanted was to escape from the important people with their agency mandates and rivalries and their personal ambitions and vanity. I had slipped away from the party after the last meeting, when they all went back to stay at the Hilton, and found myself a shabby room in a colleague's apartment.

I had been expecting some sort of reprimand for breaking ranks, but nothing more. I had followed the secretary into the office and stood at unofficial attention while the Resident Coordinator made a big show of finishing with the papers he was working on before affecting to notice me. He looked overweight, wedged into his swivel chair behind his desk. He had bushy eyebrows, darker than the greying hair above his thick horn rimmed glasses. When he looked up he had simply said 'You are insolent.'

There wasn't anything I could say to that. Later in the sleepless hours that followed I realised these words were just a ploy to throw me off guard, but at the time there just had not been anything in my mind, no reply, no way of engaging. I was out of my depth, so I had just stood in silence, refusing to be seated, while the resident coordinator told me he was planning to close down my office in Nairobi and start something new in its place, something more appropriate to the coming peace. I would be allowed to work off the last few months of my contract and then be gone.

And I had just let him speak and then taken my leave. There was nothing tactical in this. I simply had no words to say. I was outside it all, just watching, no longer participating in my own life. Now I was here, using up my final weeks by going to the field. I did not have anywhere else to go or anything to do.

I let my mind slip, out through the mosquito netting in the open doorway of the tent, through the trees on the edge of the compound, across the cattle track and down past the village, out onto the endless plain, out across the dry grasslands until it reached the swamps where the great river spread itself through a thousand channels, on through the darkness into sleep.

## 2.

*Friday evening*

The drums woke me at daybreak. They sounded near in the stillness and yet distant, the way sounds seem bigger and closer when they come from the far side of a steep valley, magnified by the walls of the cliffs around them. But here there was no valley, just a swirl of dense mist waiting for the sun to burn it off. I reached for my watch on the floor of the tent and checked the time, although I already knew it would be six o'clock. The temptation to lie a while longer came as it did every morning, whispering through the stiffness of my limbs and the ache in my back, but I knew too well that to lie prone for one minute longer than it took to work out where my flip-flops, sponge bag and towel were located would let in the restless thoughts that were not thoughts – images, feelings, anxieties, half-formed, inchoate, dark sprites that would sap my energy and take away whatever vestiges of courage remained with which to face the day. It had always been that way, year on year, and I have learnt that the only way to resist this dark suction into the abyss is to get up abruptly and confront the world of tangible objects.

I filled the bucket from the well and showered methodically, soaping and rinsing my entire body. I knew I was doing it more to make the time past than out of concern for personal hygiene, but I also knew that I needed the routine and the feeling of structure and meaning that came from obeying some rules. When I got back to my tent, John was already up and stretching, talking to Samuel, still inside his tent, as he waited for his turn in the washing area. We greeted one another and I smiled at John, determined to start the day well and encouraged by the signs of early activity. The women arrived, silently like they always did, and started to sort out the pans and plates. One of them poked around the ashes to rekindle the fire and put a large sufuria full of water directly onto the flaming logs to boil for tea.

Half an hour later when John came over from making the morning call to Loki, I had already seated myself with a tin mug of tea on the ground at my side, arranging my emergency kit before packing it into my backpack,. 'Sorting out your toys?' John posed the question with a laugh that was good natured and conversational. I knew there was no intention of malice, whatever the big Sudanese might be thinking of my little ways. He laughed a lot, always in a quiet, dignified way, always taking his time to speak, never deliberately offensive. Samuel was faster, seemingly quicker-witted, but deferential to the taller man, although you couldn't tell what this deference was due to. Maybe his age or tribal status, or his greater experience in the field, or even just physical stature. You just couldn't tell. It seemed to come naturally whenever they discussed any matter; Samuel would always speak first, quickly, without thinking, his eyes moving around fast until thy settled. Then he would look hard at John, who always stayed silent until the others had finished before giving his opinion, so that it came out like something measured and dignified with the wisdom of an elder. Perhaps he was getting ready for some role he might play in the new world they were waiting for.

But this relationship was somehow interfered with by my awkward intrusion into this landscape that they both understood so much better than I ever would. Because both of them now deferred to me. Whatever their own sense of hierarchy , they would always turn to me at the end with a look of enquiry in their eyes and when Simon spoke lengthily and smoothly, answering every question with an unhesitating string of statistics backed up with an exercise book full of dates and numbers supposedly kept over the nine months that had passed since the beginning of the year, the two Dinkas would simply listen and it would be left to me to challenge the numbers and the details and the smooth flow of words.

So I knew there was no intention of offence or mockery in John's words. The jokes about my equipment were tempered in any case by the fact that it was always my water and my snacks that we ended up sharing on the long forced marches I managed to bully them into. Squatting on my haunches, I smiled back up at the big man. 'Yes, I'm packing my toys,' I said and then added, 'What about yours? Don't forget your beans, will you?' If my emergency kit was becoming a standing joke, then so equally were the shiny lulu beans, and the contrived little exercises in participatory appraisal that John and Samuel had been taught to do. We both grinned, looking each other in the eye for the duration of a short moment of understanding, not long enough to create any sort of bond, but enough to give me a warm glow of optimism at the thought of the day ahead that had started better than any of the other days so far.

Two hours later, at a point which I judged to be halfway up the broken down track that wound its way up the side of the hill, I stopped to gulp the first refreshing drops of water that I had allowed myself from the wide-mouth plastic bottle I carried. I looked out over the vast landscape below, out across the flat lowlands of Southern Sudan extending westwards far beyond where the eye lost its ability to discern detail in the haze, with here and there low, jagged ranges poking out of the woody savannah of this South Eastern fringe of the great basin. The thought came to me that the hillside must once have been densely wooded. Now most of the trees had fallen to the axe. Ragged patches of cultivation showed through the messy brush.

I turned my gaze back down the track to look at the others. Simon and John were some three hundred yards behind me, talking as they came – more politics, I guessed without dwelling on it. John would have tuned the radio to Khartoum after signing off with Loki that morning so as to pick up the latest news on the peace process. Some way behind them Samuel was making slow progress. Fatter than the others and clearly less fit, he was finding the hill climb challenging. Keeping up the rear behind him were the two SPLM guards with their AK47's. Everywhere we went outside the village they went with us. Those were Simon's rules.

I quickly silenced a whisper of contempt that crept into my mind as I looked at them. They were not used to climbing hills and here I had the advantage on them. The heat was making the sweat pour in a continuous, irritating trickle under the brim of my hat, down from my scalp and into my eyes. But my legs and chest felt good. I felt alive and alert. If we'd set off before dark we could have done all this before the sun started bothering us, the voice said in my head. Now let them stew a bit. I would not offer to share my water until they reached the top. Let them ask for it and let them wonder why they had not brought their own.

Up ahead I could clearly discern the point where the track levelled off onto the plateau that extended eastwards across the border. Somewhere around that point the SPLA garrison were sitting, probably watching us even now. I decided to wait for the others before going on.

Simon and John came up after a few minutes. Simon smiled his most ingratiating smile, the one that went with the almost slimy voice. 'You have nice shoes,' he said, looking at the lightweight walking shoes I had bought specially for the Sudan job. They looked like trainers, but had vibram soles like walking boots. He spent a few moments admiring them and then continued 'I need a shoes like that. You can send me from Nairobi. They have it in Nairobi. You can buy it and send to me with the plane. It is easy.' He made this last pronouncement with great assurance, as though it were a done deal. There was no question of asking for the money, of course. The whole point was that it should be a donation, like everything else, something that would help him do his job. Earlier Simon had eyed my telescopic aluminium trekking stick with a covetous eye and suggested it should stay with him at the end of the mission. In other places I had noticed local chiefs and elders eying it the same way and had sensed the thought passing slowly through their minds that this new metal rod could be used to replace and improve on the ebony walking sticks that had always been their emblem of office and symbol of their power. The metal stick would be superior, for it came with new technology, with the planes that brought the vast quantities of grain and oil and would one day bring schools and clinics. The metal rod would establish them forever as the intermediaries and controllers of his new abundance.

We waited together for Samuel to catch up, drowning in sweating and wiping the unprotected bald top of his head with a white handkerchief turned grey with dust and grime. 'We're nearly there,' I told him, wanting, but not trying too hard, to sound encouraging, rather than impatient.

Samuel grinned briefly and looked hard at the other two Sudanese before sitting down heavily on a large bear rock. The three spoke together rapidly in Juba Arabic, Samuel's words coming out in gasping burst as he recovered his breath.

I guessed they were talking about me, probably resentfully, perhaps even bitterly or in anger. I did not care. I was feeling more alienated than ever from them now. They did not care about the job and took no pride in doing it well. They had no respect for truth or desire to seek out and alleviate real suffering. They just wanted the game to go on and the right side, their side, to win in the end. I had always wondered at the way they never spoke of the Khartoum government with resentment, just an amused, dispassionate interest. They knew all the leaders there, nearly as well it seemed as they knew the leaders on the SPLM side. Everyone was a player in the game, even the enemy. Even the British had once been players, the main player in fact, which was why no-one in Sudan could understand why they were not playing a bigger role now or showing more understanding of the cause of the Southern people. The British had, after all, put their mark firmly on this landscape. They had stood right here. 'This used to be a good road,' said John in his deep, slow voice. 'That's right,' said Simon. 'The British made it. Your grandfathers!' – turning to leer at me – 'They were here. You will see when we visit the garrison. They have a special hole there which the British made, a tunnel so deep you will die if you go inside.'

We started to walk again a soon as Samuel stood up, slower now, staying together to talk. 'The British were here for a long time. They had a deep tunnel with some secret inside it.' Simon was still talking about the military camp. 'We can ask the SPLA commander to show us. I know him. He is my friend.' He smiled broadly as he said this, as though to make sure the hint of vicarious power he wanted to convey with these words had been well understood.

The idea of some sort of tunnel or underground bunker seemed bizarre, though. Probably some misunderstanding converted into legend, I guessed. It would no doubt turn out to be something disappointing and mundane and I did not want to let it distract him now.

We reached the point where the track levelled off and at once became broader, more like a road. An avenue of vast mango trees opened up before us, like the plane trees lining a country road in France. 'The British planted these,' said John quietly. He spoke, as they often did in South Sudan, with a veneration for the past and a time when there had been building and roads and order, when this place, vast, empty, devastated and forgotten, had mattered, because it was part of something bigger and its future and the solution of its quandaries had mattered a lot because of that. The image came into my mind of the writer of some anonymous Anglo-Saxon poem I had once been made to read at school, confronted by the ruins of a lost civilisation destroyed by an earlier generation of his own people. There was the same feeling of a greater civilisation having existed in the past than what was present now or waited in the future. The people from the past were a race of giants.

We walked on, shaded now by the thick foliage of the mango trees. The season was past and there was no fruit on the long branches that radiated outwards in a vast, drooping symmetry. I still felt I had to confront Simon and his lists of failed crops and food needs with this evidence of his abundance. 'These trees are big,' I said. 'They must give a hell of a lot of fruit. There must be fruit for everyone during the season, don't you think?' I let my question hang for a second and then added before Simon could retort: 'Who gets to pick the fruit anyway? Who owns the trees? Who has the right?'

Simon laughed his usual laugh, slick and supercilious. 'Everyone has the right to pick the fruit,' he said. 'But different people own the trees. They know themselves whose is which.' The contradiction in these two statements made it impossible to understand whether the community as a whole benefited from the fruit. That was the way it always was. There was always ambivalence and contradiction throughout the whole system. It was never a case of a clearly defined set of data implying something else equally clearly defined, but always a hazy mixture of hearsay, misrepresentation and supposition. Underlying it all there was something fundamental, a badness and a wrong that was evident everywhere, but like an undiagnosed illness it was never possible to prescribe the cure. They talked about the endless years of conflict, the absence of development, of schools or roads or clinics, of children with guns, endless small scale displacements, but somehow it had to be fitted onto the deeper patterns of life in the toic, the routine movement with the cattle year in year out, the droughts and floods and the rhythms of a cruel nature, a hard life on the edge that had persisted longer than memory, or history, or politics. Or mango trees, come to that. They were as peripheral as the men who had planted them.

'We had better note that in our table, though,' I said, turning to John and Samuel, frowning to show that I was in earnest and then looking round to Simon to ensure he too had heard.

We had agreed that our main objective in climbing up to the plateau would be to interview the minority ethnic communities who lived up there. Simon had agreed to arrange a meeting with a group of Kachipo. They were already sitting on the ground in the small market place, huddled together and silent, small people compared to the Dinkas, highland goat-rearers, not cattle people. The women had lip-plates and long, pendant earlobes that had been plugged and stretched over a lifetime. They had the look that comes from prolonged hunger, ragged and emaciated without any clear expression on their faces or in their eyes.

They had left a long, narrow fallen tree branch facing them for us - their guests - to sit on. I squatted down and lowered myself onto it, feeling the thin, gnarled wooden bar dig sharply into the flesh of my buttocks. It occurred to me that ground would have made a better seat, but I was here now, sitting, and had better stay that way. John and Samuel looked sideways at me along the branch. Simon grinned and started to talk in Murle to the Kachipo.

I let my eyes travel round the circle of blank faces. Who were these people, how far had they come, how long had they waited for us to show up, and what did they really think this strange meeting was all about? These people were the real mystery, doubly isolated by language, strangers even to the Sudanese. I doubted they would benefit from any relief supplies, in any case. The distributions took place down below at the airstrip and they never went down there.

On the other hand, their misery, real or imagined, was useful to Simon in building his case for this year's quota and so he had been ready enough to come up here with the team and to set up this meeting. But what was he saying to them now? What were his real words, not what he claimed to be saying? And what were these people trying to tell their visitors? An old woman became suddenly animated, talking fast and raising her voice.

'What is she saying?' I asked Simon. I spoke sharply. I was irritated by the way Simon seemed to be condescending to these people, as thought they were inferior to him and by the way my own inability to speak directly to them cut them off from me and made it impossible to tell if I had heard anything of what they really had to say.

'She is talking her language,' said Simon, smiling, as though he were talking to a child or a simpleton.

'Well get someone to tell you what she is saying.'

The woman talked on for several minutes and then fell silent, sitting back, her face expressionless once more. I looked around the circle, expecting one of the others to translate, then looking at Simon again.

But no-one translated. The woman's words remained cloaked in the mystery of her tongue and her hilltop world, stretching away into the east, from where a cold gust of wind rustled the leaves above our heads. I looked at her and felt very far away from her and from that world of hers. The urgency of her words, spoken in her hidden tongue, carried no meaning for me. I was outside her anxiety, her pain, her hope and her despair. I felt a surge of the yearning inside that had turned me into a rootless being, shifting from one place to another, always restless and always destined to discover over again that when I got to wherever I was going I would find nothing of what I thought I was looking for. Right now the feeling told me that maybe if I could only find the bigness of imagination to start walking east across the hills, to walk and walk until I came to an Ethiopia that felt suddenly like home, I might find something, but I knew at the same instant that the urge to go there came without any deeper sense of purpose. It wouldn't achieve anything. I simply felt sad and aware that I was not going to help the woman or her people. I would never even know how far she had come from and how long it had taken her to get to the bare patch of ground under the mango trees.

A memory came into my mind the way they always do, unannounced and unexpected, triggered by some chance coincidence of sight, sound or sense, sharp and vivid with the startling brightness of a vision. We were sitting on a rug on top of a bare mountain in Shewa, gazing out over the wide, silent landscape. The ponies were cropping the short grass nearby. Far below a farmer was winnowing a golden cloud of t'eff outside his tumble-down wooden farmstead. The tin roof gleamed in the sun. She looked across at me, did not say anything, but shivered as the gust caught us. She never did speak in these memories. I had forgotten the sound of her voice, anyway, a long time before.

A second gust of wind, instantly cool on the overheated skin of my face, brought my mind back abruptly to the present. There was nothing more to say, it seemed. The circle was silent. I reached into my pack and pulled out the packet of biscuits and the large plastic bag of peanuts which I had brought with me. I opened them and passed them round, beginning with the old woman who had spoken last.

When the food had all been shared out and consumed I stood up, rubbing the numbness out of my buttocks and stretching. I looked down at Simon, who was still sitting while he adjusted a cheap plastic-framed pair of sunglasses that he had pulled out of the breast pocket of his shirt. 'Who else is there up here?' I asked.

'The IDPs are here as well as down below,' said John. There are so many Dinkas who have come back from Ethiopia.'
I knew about them, of course. It had been in the briefing. No-one knew how many there were. In any case they came and went. Some were returning refugees, as John had said, but others were just here, because people had been showing up in strange places since the conflict started. In the early days I had once had the idea of starting a systematic mapping of the whole situation, sorting out the different pockets of displaced and transient people scattered across the South, but the idea had not got very far. The inter-agency task force had met a few times, but they had never been able to agree on parameters or criteria for sharing data or making maps. They had sat in the conference room at the Landmark Hotel in Westlands and talked, people from Khartoum, from Loki, from Rumbek, together with those from Nairobi. They had been happy to talk. Everyone liked to talk. And in the end I had given up and let it fade away, like everything else I had

tried. Now I was here, failing to make sense of all the numbers and the things they were telling me and the bits and pieces my own eyes could see. I had known that it would be that way and yet I had come. In the end I had not really cared about that. I had come in order to go for a walk in the bush, to be part of that other place, to feel the sun and gaze at the shimmering landscape, to smell the smoke of the fire and hear the frogs in the night and the drums at dawn and the high treble voices of the boys singing at the start of their school day in the schools without books. I had come because there was nowhere else I could go and I was as restless as I was tired.

The others got up slowly and we walked on, leaving the Kachipo still seated in silence. Beyond the market the tree-lined road gave way to a large open square. On one side of it there was a large new looking wooden building with a tin roof. Ahead a man wearing a welding mask that hid his face so that you could not tell if he was a local or a foreigner, was standing on a ladder welding an iron girder to complete the skeleton of what would by local standards be a substantial building. 'He is the priest,' said Simon. 'Father Severino.'

We reached the foot of the ladder. A tall, thin South Sudanese wearing a tank-top that emphasised the long powerful muscles of his glistening arms was holding it steady. Another stood to one side waiting to pass a metal girder up. The welder removed the mask from his face and looked down at us. 'Hello,' he said, without smiling or waiting for introductions. 'We are building the church. I have to do it myself, as you can see.' His voice was serious and tired. He looked young, no older than thirty, dark haired and slightly dark skinned, probably Spanish or Latin American. 'Go and see the school,' he added, still without smiling or showing any inclination to welcome us. 'Sister Lucy is there. I will be finished here soon.'

A hundred yards away there was a single storey wooden building with a thatched roof. It was large and solid. It looked new. Between it and where we were standing the grass was short, with the almost manicured look of a parade ground. It all looked like the good schools did, the ones built with hope and belief and run by teachers who taught like evangelists of the cult of knowledge, not the small, hopeless, tumble down converted huts I had seen everywhere else in Sudan, but a real school, like you might find in Kenya.

A woman wearing a headscarf and plain white dress that proclaimed her to be the bride of Christ came out as we approached. She was large in the way the pastoral people got once modern life took away their leanness. She wore dark-framed glasses with big, ugly lenses that gave her face a heavy, unfriendly look. I noticed the shoes she was wearing on her large, pastoralist feet were white, like her dress and headscarf. The whiteness drew my eye. The world was barefoot and she had white shoes. The shoes made her different, like my own white skin. She looked strong, and sure of herself and maybe, the meanness inside my mind whispered, the shoes helped with that, but when she spoke her voice was the voice of one of those teachers who can control a class without raising their voice, just with a look, a small change in the line of the mouth, the slightest movement of an outstretched hand.

When I was a small child I had a teacher like that in my primary school in the village where I grew up out in the Fens. She used to take us for nature walks and tell us the names of the flowers and plants and what the country people had used them for in the old days, the times that in my young child's mind were always associated with the televised episodes of Dickens' novels that paraded a dark world of candle-lit child abuse through the later stages of Sunday afternoons that I would spend in front of the television set after getting home from the obligatory family walk. People said she was a witch.

'I am Sister Lucy,' she said. 'I came here with Father Severino last year. I am from Uganda originally. I stayed here alone when he went to get the building materials. He brought them all the way from Kenya in a lorry.' She sounded proud saying this, and more so when she added 'We are alone here. The diocese does not help. They have forgotten us.'

'Which diocese?' I asked, without knowing why this detail should interest me.

'Torit,' she said. 'It is far from here. I came with the Father from Uganda. Some of the displaced people here have relatives and family in Uganda or in Labone near the border.'

I had been to the huge camps in Labone , on the edge of the bamboo forested hills, where one of the bigger NGOs was experimenting with turning pastoralists into maize-farmers. Fear of the LRA kept the people huddled together in a sprawling township of grass huts in the middle of the crop fields they had planted, leaving the forest untouched, as though the murderous child soldiers were forest rangers, killing and maiming in the name of biodiversity and global public goods, in the pay of some overseas conservation group. That had been the year before, at the time of the survey of IDPs that ultimately came to nothing.

Children were filing out in silence, two by two like choir boys. Almost all of them were boys with just a handful of girls sprinkled among them. They all had uniforms, white shirts and blue shorts or skirts, and all were bare-foot. The clothes were clean and their eyes were very bright, carrying the same hope you always saw in the eyes of children wearing school uniforms. It seemed to be expecting something from me and it made me squirm inside at the vanity that crept into my mind and told me that they were looking to me for a salvation I could not bring.

'They want to sing for you,' said Sister Lucy. I felt sure she was aware of my awkwardness and revelled in it. There was a triumphant note, or maybe an overtone of defiance in her voice that came through to me like outright hostility, though maybe I just imagined it because the children were making me feel bad about myself with their fragile, bright-eyed hope. I smiled and steadied myself, straightening my body from the slack-spined slouch the heat always seemed to crumple it into.

They sang the boy scout song. I knew they would before they started. School children always sang it in Southern Sudan, the song about clapping your hands if you were happy and you knew it. They seemed happy, in spite of everything. They clapped their hands and sang their hearts out in shrill, tuneful voices, the same voices I had heard in other villages deep among the reed beds and buried in the morning mists down in the swamp and out across the flat grassland sea that had no further shore.

When the song was over they stopped dead and there was silence in which the visitors and the children looked at each other, shy and wary, unsure about what should happen next. Sister Lucy looked at everyone for a while, saying nothing, but letting the silence grow naturally in the space left when the singing voices stopped, until it became imbued with something more than the absence of words and the absence of the constant background din of the world, and the whisper of the slight breeze through the net-like web of leaves of the thorny acacia trees that bordered the parade ground became an insistent invitation to lonely memory and despair.

I could tell she was waiting to judge the moment when sufficient calm had been restored after the excitement of the music. Then she spoke, quietly and strongly again, to invite us to come with her to look around. She made sure we saw everything, every identical classroom with its simple wooden desk and bench units, blackboard and chalk. There was time, the way there always is when you let yourself enter the African world.

At the end she showed us her small collection of Ugandan text books, exercise books and
 pencils. I held an empty, lined notebook in my hand and felt its weight bear down on my spirit so that I suddenly found I wanted to confess to her and to everyone else that from the very outset I had been stupidly – more than that, boorishly - at fault in my impatience with John and Samuel down in the SRRC campsite each morning. I had been itching to get out and get on with the thing that was making me itch, the foolish, futile activities I insisted on every day as a way of justifying our presence – my presence - here in this place that did not belong to the way I did things and, more than that, as a way of exorcising the demons that found me every night.

The urge to deprecate myself subsided quickly enough, leaving in its place a need to make some sort of friendly gesture to the colleagues I had abused, as though the good things I was seeing might be offering me a chance of grace. I looked over at them, nodding my head in appreciation of what Sister Lucy was saying and trying to share the feeling with them. I wanted to say something positive and encouraging, something flowing from the lightness that was in me for a moment, but Sister Lucy spoke before I could, asking in her cold, soft voice, tinged now with a flat-toned disdain that anticipated an unsatisfactory answer, whether the UN could help with school supplies.

'You can see how little we have,' she said, holding up one of the books. 'But we have more than a hundred children in this school and it is their only hope. You see how they want to be in school.'

I looked at the rows of children, still standing at attention behind the small wooden desks. It was hot and stuffy in the room and I was glad when Sister Lucy told them they could sit down.

'It is a very good school,' said Simon suddenly, stepping forward in front of the rest of the group to place himself between us and Sister Lucy. 'Very good. We need a school like this down below too. I have asked Father Severino.'

'We do not have anyone to run it,' said Sister Lucy firmly. Her clear, educated accent jarred against Simon's babbling delivery and reasserted the silence. I could feel her strength. She was in control here and she had the measure of Simon.

She took us outside again and showed us the well-kept vegetable garden beyond the school room. 'We grow food for the children,' she said. 'We provide them with one meal each day.'

'Whose children are they?' I asked.

Simon took a step forward again with the same clear intention of interposing himself between us, speaking fast so as to answer the question before Sister Lucy could. 'There are many IDPs here,' he said. 'They are Dinkas. They came back from Ethiopia. They belong to Bor county, but they could stay here. The school is for them. That is why we need another school down below.' He grinned.

'Do you also have Kachipo children,' I asked, addressing myself very deliberately to Sister Lucy. 'And Murle?'

'Yes,' she said. 'There are a few Kachipo. More Murle. There are more of them. The Kachipo come from far.' She signalled with her eyes towards the East, where the track lead through the straggle of huts at the end of the village and out into the hills beyond. Then she added: 'We are here for all who want, but some are more interested than others and it is difficult for the girls.' I looked again at the rows of children, making a mental headcount of boys and girls, confirming yet again the fact, as predictable as a Unicef report, that the boys far outnumbered the girls.

Then Simon said 'Let us go and see if Father Severino has finished.'

Looking across the field we could see the priest. He had climbed down from the ladder and was talking to the two large Sudanese men who were helping him, as he handed his goggles and the welding torch to them. They trundled the equipment away leaving him alone as we approached.

'I'm sorry,' he said. 'I had to finish that job. I have to do it myself, you see.' He repeated these words from their first meeting. His voice sounded tired and the tiredness showed in his unsmiling face. His shirt was soaked with the sweat that was still dripping from his wavy, black hair down onto the frayed collar. He wiped the back of his neck with his hand and then looked long and hard at his visitors, at ease with the silence he had created, a man doing a job and weary beyond caring for the niceties of social interaction.

The metal girders were in place now, framing the rectangular space that would be the church and the triangular prism of the roof. I let my eyes wander over the metal skeleton, wondering where the priest had acquired the practical skills for what he was doing, envying that and envying the courage that could hold a man to stay and work in such a place without support. When the priest spoke again, I noticed his voice. There was a softness in it that invited confidence, a softness that was not weak, but kind. By contrast my own voice seemed to have lost so much that could be counted attractive, degenerating into the grating growl of an angry man without an audience, growing old and wondering where he was.

'You've seen the school,' the priest was saying. 'We built that first. We had to build that ourselves, too. We have done everything ourselves. I brought everything we have in my truck. I drove it all up from Nairobi last month.'

'Yes, the sister told us,' I replied. I could feel something in his voice that I had not felt for a long time, something akin to eagerness or enthusiasm. The lethargy that draped itself over every effort and every endeavour in this forsaken land had not tainted this man; there was an energy emanating from his tired eyes and sweaty, muscular body that was difficult to resist, like finding the only other castaway on an island is someone endowed with a sincerity that makes him immediately someone you could talk to and be sure the answers he gave would be true, someone who could guide this little band that was all I and my two team-mates amounted to, hopelessly out of our depth as we were. Or at least help us see if we were getting things right.

At the same time I felt another feeling growing like a tune in negative counterpoint to the good feeling, a resentment, mean and pinched, coupled with an envy that I knew to be childish and spiteful for someone who must have a sense of purpose strong enough to impel him to come all the way to this place and take it for his own and, once arrived, to just get on with doing things, not questioning, examining, criticising in the way that I did – always from the outside -, but simply being what he was and part of the things he did, which justified everything and killed the need to think too hard.

I needed to break the ugly spell that was growing inside and around me. Speaking fast so as to get through with it before anyone interrupted or anything could happen to distract their attention, I introduced the team and explained why we had come.

I started with the assumption I always made when talking to NGO field staff or SRRC officials and village chiefs, that I was just running over familiar ground. But I was wrong in this. He had not heard about any of the things that defined us and our world - about the annual needs assessment, or about Operation Lifeline Sudan, or the planes and the briefing and the wild weekend parties at Loki, - and he did not have much idea about the United Nations Agencies and NGO's they represented. He had come here alone. This was his mission – his and Sister Lucy's. They were here to help the people who no-one else was helping. This was his parish in a forgotten corner of the diocese of Torit. The comings and goings of the agencies and the NGOs and the whole self-justifying business of humanitarian assistance passed them by.

'I went to Torit to see the bishop,' he said and there was sadness and frustration in his voice. 'But he was away on a tour of the United States and nobody was interested.' For a moment he seemed to lose himself in a silent, bitter contemplation of the lonely struggle he had pursued, until the silence was broken by Simon.

'We know Father Severino,' he said, turning to smile at me. 'The SRRC appreciated the school he has made here. We are waiting for a new school down below in our village. We know his work is good. We will support him.'

The priest smiled at him. It was a knowing, slightly forced smile, the smile of a man who has been working hard, but knows his labours will not get him anywhere if he does not make his peace with the ones who have the power, however little of it and however local. Then he turned back and brightened. 'You could help us, then, if you are the United Nations,' he said. 'We need school books. You saw the school. There is no equipment.'

'Yes of course.' It was always easy to say this. 'It will be in the report. I'll get all the figures for school age children and make sure it is there.'

Too easy to say and do, I knew. To put something in a report, even to send a note directly to the UNICEF office would not avail much. But that was all I could do, after all. It did not seem much of a justification for why I was here. The dissatisfaction that was taking me downwards through the self-questioning insomnia in the insect-shrill nights was wrapped up in this – a useless life lived pointlessly on the edge of every opportunity to create, to do, to do something that might make a difference, like someone who could come to a place like this and take it as his parish, build schools, help people, protect them, get to know them, care for them, see faces where he and his kind saw only numbers. It seemed the secret was locked up in this; that Father Severino was an actor on this stage; that he had the self-belief to say 'I don't like what I see' and them to change it with his own hands against the odds. It did not finish there, I knew, but I was aware that there was something I wanted here, something that was pulling me back from the edge of a dark and blank place. I felt a great desire to talk more with the priest, but not now, here with the others; another time, alone. 'Like confession,' I thought and smiled to myself without humour.

'I am sorry I cannot invite you to eat with us,' said Father Severino. He was smiling now in a different way, relaxed, it seemed, having made his request for help. 'I have to visit my parish. There are some women who are sick and I will go with Sister Lucy to see them.'

The others each shook hands with the priest and began to walk back towards the entrance to the village. I had deliberately hung back so that I would be the last. 'Father Severino,' I said, as he held out his hand. 'I'd like to talk some more. Will you have time?' The words seemed awkward, like the words of a small boy to an unfamiliar adult.

The priest did not answer immediately, as though he knew too well that time cannot be pinned down in this way. Then he asked 'Are you staying in the village below?'

'Yes, we're camped in the SRRC compound.'

'Well, we are coming down tomorrow. I have work with the people there and then there is a Jiye village I must visit. It is quite far from here. We will go the following day. Maybe you would like to come? You will see these people. You'll see they have nothing. They need any help they can get, even the little that we are able to do.'

The invitation, simple and direct, came as a surprise, like all the best gifts, to offer me a ray of hope that I might yet turn things around and achieve something meaningful out of the mess that was my portion. I did not hesitate. 'Yes, I would like to come along, Father Severino,' I said. 'It will be very useful.'

It felt awkward to call this man, younger than myself, 'Father', but I wanted to show deference now, something akin to what my Sudanese colleagues had been showing to me so far. I did not know, though, why I had added the thing about it being useful. It had just come out, straight our from the need to justify everything in terms of utility, which was the disguise I used to hide any sign of ulterior, more personal motive – interest in my surroundings or in the customs and languages of people seldom visited, pleasure in the adventure. There was no enjoyment permitted in what I did. It was about justification and it therefore had to be grim and hard.

The priest smiled at me and I felt a brief glow, a stronger return of the feelings I had felt at the beginning, of likeness and understanding that is innate and recognises one of its own. Then the priest said 'I'll come and find you at around four o'clock.'

'Tea time,' I said.

The priest looked puzzled at this.

'I'm English,' I said, as though that explained anything. 'I'll drink tea. Maybe you'll have coffee.'

'Yes...'

His voice trailed away involuntarily, leaving a space to be filled by awkwardness. I spoke again, quickly to keep the embarrassment stillborn, asking, 'Where are you from, Father Severino?'

'Mexico.'

'It's a long way to come.'

'Yes, but I always wanted to work in Africa. Since I became a priest. This is my calling.'

To talk without any apparent embarrassment about a 'calling' was not part of the world I lived and worked in. It placed me under the lintel of a world I did not want to enter, but at a time when the need for company might drive me forward. Instinctively I uttered the words that would close the conversation down for the time being, while closing nothing off: 'We'll talk some more tomorrow.'

'Yes, I can tell you about the rest of our plans. I am sure you can help.' The priest's eyes met mine, earnest and dark. I turned brusquely and hurried to join the others.

The SPLA camp was situated on the edge of a cliff that overshadowed the settlement and from where it looked out beyond to the ill-defined hazy western horizon where the lowlands merged with the sky. The barracks and other installations were invisible from the track as we approached, but two soldiers stood, tall and thin in faded fatigues, waiting for us by the rusty painted sign at the entrance.

'The commander is waiting for us,' said Simon. 'You can ask him about the British cave. But be careful here.'

Simon had a way of repeating points he had made earlier on, as though he felt a need to drum them in, over and over again. Now he made it feel as if coming here had been the whole reason for climbing the hill. It irritated me, like the sweat that dripped down onto my nose from my hair. A vicious remark came into my mouth but I chewed it down. I did not want to start something now that might disrupt the whole exercise. My mind was filling with new possibilities, not yet defined but taking shaped and rooted in something new, like so many other brief inspirations there had been before that had eventually foundered on indifference and failure of spirit in one form or another.

We came to a small hut with its door left open to let the breeze in. The soldiers stood back to let us enter. I noticed the expressions on their faces were hard, like dried masks – the expressionless mask of the combat-hardened, beings from another world temporarily inactive, but potentially very dangerous. A smell of stale sweat emanating from the interior seemed to cling to them as though it owned and defined them.

Inside an old man in a uniform as faded as that of the guards was sitting behind a desk facing the open door. The close cropped hair that remained around his temples was grey turning to white. He listened while Simon introduced our party. Then he reached across his small desk and shook the hand of each one of us in turn, slowly without smiling.

'This was the first camp we set up when we re-took our land,' he said. He looked closely at me, the foreigner. 'Are you British?' he asked.

'Yes.'

'This was a British camp, you know.'

'Yes, Simon told me.'

'The British were here for a long time. They grew coffee.'

'We saw the mango trees they planted.'

'They did a lot.' I was sure I could detect a hint of admiration in the old man's voice, like that of a dark age warrior seeing the shadows of departed legions still haunting the chaos of the present. He paused and allowed the silence to grow beyond what was confortable, then he spoke for a long time with Simon and the others in Juba Arabic, never raising his voice, controlling the conversation without moving, asking questions and then speaking slowly, calmly, giving orders with eyes that matched his words in their slow deliberate movement from one face to another.

I could pick out some of what they were saying. The bits I understood seemed routine – details of where we were going, where we were from. But when the commander noticed that I was trying to follow their talk, he paused and looked round slowly to make eye contact. Then in the same unhurried voice he said 'I am sorry, perhaps we should speak English.'

I could not decipher the tone of this remark. The softness of the commander's voice gave no scope for interpretation. Perhaps there was irony in his words or anger disguised as irony, but then again he might just as easily have been indulging in the same game as Simon. There was no way to tell and in that dangerous uncertainty the best way forward – that much at least I knew - was to stay polite. 'It's ok. My colleagues can translate, if you prefer.'

'That is not necessary. But now tell me, is it your plan to go far from Boma? Brother Simon tells me you like to move around and see things for yourself.'

'No,' I said. I did not like the thought of Brother Simon telling anything about me, though that was probably part of what he had been doing just now. No doubt he had been describing me as an interloper, a man who asked too much and went turning over stones, refusing to accept what he was told. 'We already visited some villages nearby.' Then it occurred to me to ask 'Why? Is there a problem somewhere?'

'No,' said the commander. 'There is not. Or you would not even be here.' He spoke in the same calm, measured way, so unlike Simon's fast, over-friendly manner. And where the latter bred only distrust and a sense of irritation reverting to a superiority that verged on something racial and deeply atavistic, this calm was the simple expression of a will that would not be opposed.

'If you go far from Boma,' he said. 'It is not possible to be sure. There has been some trouble between the Toposa and the Jiye. Cattle raids. There was a bad one quite recently. It would be dangerous down that way, towards the south.'

'The road to Loki is closed,' said John. 'WFP is not bringing anything by road.'

'We will not be travelling so far,' said Simon with a smile. 'We do not have a vehicle, everywhere is walking. They are tired, you can see!' He laughed in his usual irritating, superior way, allowing the laugh to make it clear that he despised the ability of the foreigner to walk through the grasslands and the heat. The commander nodded his head silently and then stood up to end the interview, reaching out across the desk to shake our hands again.

At this point I knew things had gone well. There would be no objection to what we were doing and we would not be impeded or told to leave. There was no need to say anything else and yet nothing had been said and there was a frustration in that that pushed me to bring out the things that could have just been left on one side to gather dust. Somehow that would have been another victory for Simon and the irritation I felt with the way whenever the conversation became something more than trivial it always slipped behind the barrier of language would have grown to torment me beyond what I could bear.

As the commander turned to me, I said, 'Can I ask you one other thing, Commander,' before we go? Simon said there was something strange, a tunnel.' I spoke in loud voice, giving special emphasis to Simon's name and looking at him as I said it.

For a moment the commander frowned. Simon was still smiling and said something to him in Juba Arabic, which caused his facial muscles to relax. 'Ah yes,' he said. 'Do you want to see?'

He led us outside and back past the sentries onto a small track through the bushes that grew densely here, not cropped by any animals. After some twenty yards we turned abruptly to one side and started to descent the face of the cliff on a narrow path that led us hopping from boulder to boulder. Twenty yards further on we stopped before a wide fissure in the rock face.

The commander leaned forward into the interior. 'It is deep and very dark,' he said. 'Do you have a battery?'

I set my back pack on the ground, unzipped a side pocket and took out the small electric torch. When I turned it on its feeble beam lost itself in the gloom of a cave that I could see was much bigger than the entrance had suggested. There was no roof and no floor beyond the initial slope that led to a sudden downward plunge into a dark void. Beyond that there was no final wall, just darkness. The place held us, still and silent, menacing with the mystery of darkness and the sudden cooling that three paces forward brought, turning the sweat on the inside of our shirts run into a cold, unpleasant trickle.

'The tunnel starts at the back,' said the commander quietly. 'They tell me some people have gone inside and have not come back. My men are frightened of this place.'

'Have you been inside yourself?' I asked.

'I do not fear,' said the commander. 'I have fought in every battle of this war. I have killed many men and I have watched men die. I have no fear. But you should have fear, you should. You are far from home. If you were here alone you would be very far, very far.' For a moment he was silent as the darkness grew around them and the memory of the sun's glare faded. When he spoke again his voice seemed to come from very close behind, as though he were whispering: 'You know there used to be a rumour that we threw the bodies in here after we killed people. But it is just a rumour.' In the darkness of the cave mouth his face was a shadow.

I stared into the gloom, feeling the commander's breath close to my ear in the dark. For a moment all that was real was the immense distance that separated me from the world I came from. It weighed on me as though I were an astronaut alone in space, beyond all contact, help or comfort from the home that might no longer even exist.

Then the moment passed. The commander turned back towards the light. 'I think it is time for you to leave,' he said. 'You should stay away from places like this, places that may be bad. Stay where it is safe.'

He stepped back out into the sunlight and the others all followed. 'The British had some poison there,' said Simon as we emerged, 'That is why they say you will die if you go inside.'

No-one said anything in response to this, so he continued on different tack . 'People come here looking for gold. The rains wash it down from the rocks and the hills and people find gold in the rivers at the bottom.'

'Yes,' said Samuel suddenly joining in, as though Simon had selected a theme that would restore harmony. 'The young men from Kakuma come here in the season to look for gold in the rivers.'

It seemed inconceivable that they would just set out and walk across the hostile miles of desert from the refugee camp in Northern Kenya, but I knew it could easily be true. People were moving all the time, just as they always had been, and the war was just a background canvass for this movement, sometimes provoking it, sometimes irrelevant to it, but always there. In Labone I had been told that the young men from Kakuma refugee camp would walk all the way up there in the season of green maize in order to feast on the succulent cobs. Maybe that was how they built their strength for the gold prospecting in the badlands around Boma. Maybe they just wandered around in a seasonal circle between these places.

'There was a Norwegian once with a special machine,' said Simon. 'He was looking for gold.'

'Did he find any?'

'Oh yes. There is much gold. This land is very rich, so very rich, and one day we shall benefit, not just the foreigners and the government in Khartoum. They have always come to steal our riches. They kill and displace our people. But soon the peace will come and then in the New Sudan we will safeguard our own resources. We will be rich and strong.'
He broke off and looked around, like a politician gauging the reaction of his audience after making a speech.

The expression on the commander's face did not change and he said nothing. Simon stopped talking. The commander took my hand again as though in a final goodbye handshake, but his grip did not slacken after the one or two seconds a handshake should take. Instead I felt the strong fingers tighten their grip around my own, like a python squeezing the life out of a small rodent.

The commander looked into my eyes in a steady, unsmiling gaze. 'If the government of Khartoum thought there were resources here,' he said quietly, 'They would send their militias down from the Nuer lands to turn this place into a warzone where nobody can live safely and the civilians die or run. Then the Chinese would come with military escorts...' He paused for a moment, still looking hard and unblinking into my eyes, as though he thought he could read what was going on in my mind in response to what he was saying. 'It is good that they do not know. The people can live in peace...'

He released my hand. Everyone remained silent for a long minute during which the only sound was the rustling of the wind through the long dry grass and the brittle, thorny branches of the acacias outside.

### 3.

*Saturday night*
It was slow going back down the hill. Everyone was tired and the day was still hot. Near the entrance to the SRRC compound there was a group of Jiye, mostly old men and women, sitting under a tree to smoke. Each one had a kind of rustic sheesha made out of a gourd with a bamboo cane for the mouthpiece. They were wrapped in faded, dirty blankets, like Maasai without the glitz and the posing they put on for the tourists to photograph. Simon called out to them from twenty yards' distance and then, with that mocking, over-simplifying tourist guide style he seemed to have perfected just in order to irritate me, turned to explain that he had summoned the Jiye from their village somewhere far out on the plain so that there would be no need for the visitors to over-exert themselves . They could answer every question here.

I was sure this was a pre-emptive move, set up to prevent prying eyes from going down there into the frying pan heat where the waving grass seemed to melt like butter into the distant horizon. I was tired, I realised, almost too tired to think straight, but a smile flickered inside my mind at the thought of Father Severino and his pick-up truck. It would take me easily out across the empty reaches, bumping down the track that was now fading into the sunset. Simon would be an irrelevance to that enterprise. I would not even need to take him along to interpret.

For now, though, I had to concentrate on this sad little group. They had a lot to say in reply to the standard questions. They took their time and they took turns to speak, but as always I felt cut off by Simon's free translations and the heavy-handed way he organised the interview. Whatever I might want to ask and whatever they might want to have me hear would have to pass through him and in the end there could be no subtlety in questions asked this way and no certainty in the replies. It did not even have to mean he was re-wording or distorting what they said in that awkward, artificial moment where we were actors in a grotesque tableau portraying the awkward meeting of the naïve, alien philanthropist with the intended beneficiaries of his largesse. In the end all this could do was encourage them to paint as desperate a picture as they could so that their needs would be taken care of by the plane. And I could see, with a clarity that had been growing in my eyes and in my understanding since the very first naïve and wide-eye flight I had taken from Loki into the field, that in the end this would destroy their will to fend themselves more surely than the worst of droughts or massacres and that made it all just part of the process of bringing them into the ant-hill.

One of the younger women was holding a small child on her knee, breastfeeding it as she spoke. She had a thin face with dedicate features and wore her hair tightly braided against her head. I wondered what she was really saying. Perhaps it would have made a difference if I could only have understood her words directly.

Squatting next to the woman was a man with a face that had been ritually scarred with a row of little dots around his eyes. Simon smiled his supercilious smile and announced that this man had attended some adult education classes and could speak a little English. Then he turned to him like a circus ring-master who has just introduced a new star act. A look of agitation appeared in the man's eyes. He was concentrating hard, focusing effort into memory. Until with immense effort he brought the sound out from deep inside his chest, one word, carefully and slowly articulated: 'Goodbye'.

The interview was over. The sudden roar of a plane's engine low over head set the whole group running towards the airstrip. It was always like that, sudden and loud, as though appearing out of nowhere or puncturing through the fabric of space from another dimension. I looked up and read the words Operation Lifeline Sudan painted along the white fuselage of the Caravan turning low above the trees as it made its inspection circuit prior to landing.

No-one had told me about this flight. They must have known about it from the morning radio call, but it hadn't seemed worth sharing with me. The thought of this gratuitous act of shutting me out added fuel to my irritation, but it was overwhelmed at once by the fatigue that hit me again with a vicious, gratuitous violence, like a cudgel smashing against my legs and back. I ached throughout my body and limbs, but more than that I felt the sinking of my spirits, plunging towards the empty depths where my mind, naked and alone, would face its daily wrestle with the futility of everything I had ever done.

It could always be counted on, this deadly feeling, usually at the time when the light was fading, when I was physically and mentally tired and tired also in spirit, the time when it would occur to me that the other fatigue was pointless, unjustified by achievement or hope. I hung behind as my colleagues set off for the airstrip with Simon. The sun was spread out in a broken egg melodrama across the western sky, darkening through mauve and indigo above my head. I gazed at it for a few moments, glad to put some distance between myself and my tormentor. I wished I had brought some cigarettes. I only ever smoked when I was out on mission or drunk. This time around I had tried to resist, but now I found myself wishing I hadn't.

Of course, there was nothing for it. I might as well just get on with things. I only had to get through this evening and then tomorrow there would be the priest and the prospect of the drive. It would be a victory, a great escape, and I would sit next to Father Severino and hear what he had to say and hope that somehow that would give me the true picture.

I set off at last to follow the others, self-consciously raising my head and straightening my back.

The plane only stayed on the ground for two minutes, long enough for a single small figure to emerge in the isolation of the engine's unceasing roar and get his gear out of the cargo section in the quiet, unobtrusive way of those who have travelled a lot in the bush. As I came over to join them, John explained that the newcomer was a food monitor from WFP, sent to prepare for a Hercules drop. His name was Daniel. John knew him, of course. He knew everyone in the WFP team.

The man was a Kenyan. He was small and sharp-looking next to the big, slow Sudanese. He looked like a city boy from Nairobi, slick and cool, out of place in the toic. He jumped with practiced ease from the open door of the taxi-ing plane and jogged to the edge of the runway. Behind him the plane reached the end of the runway and turned to take off, fast, without stopping, racing to get back to Loki before nightfall.

Later, in the dark, as they ate the cabbage stew and gooey rice cooked up by the silent women, I overheard the others talking. They were speaking in English for Daniel's benefit, but in fact Daniel was doing most of the talking anyway. It seemed he wanted to talk, the way lonely people who do not like being alone need to talk when they meet other people, and he was flippant, almost arrogant, in his way of speaking, as though he had been restored through finding the company he had craved to something beyond his baseline self.

He talked most about sex. His main theme was how easy it was to come to a comfortable temporary arrangement with a fellow aid-worker as homesick and bored as yourself in this empty land, stuck in one of the WFP or Unicef bases, far from family, lonely, bored. It was the easiest and most natural thing to just start something. He laughed a lot as he talked. He smoked a lot, too – Marlboros bought in Loki or Nairobi, not the cheap Ethiopian Nyalas that were all you could get out here.

Samuel was laughing from time to time, at the points where he was meant to, but his laughter sounded uneasy. Maybe he was troubled because he was working for a Christian organisation. He made a quiet, unconvincing comment about the Bible saying you should be faithful to your spouse and lowered his eyes with a sidelong look to John for support. But John had lowered his eyes and it made it look as though he and Samuel were sharing some dirty secrets in their past, now reformed and put behind, but still threatening to catch up with them at times like these.

I left them early and went to my tent, tired and hoping that sleep would come quickly for once. I checked the Thuraya before switching off my torch and lying down. I thought how good it was to have a sat phone. It was like having a lifeline to the real world, the one chance to get reeled back up if diving down here in the depths ever got out of hand.

It would have been better still if there had been someone to phone out there beyond the starlit horizon.

A hyena let out a high, jabbering call. I sat on my camp bed and listened. The jokey conversation continued, mostly Daniel's voice, too loud and laughing hard and raucous, interspersed occasionally with the deep, quiet rumble of John's bass or Samuel, higher pitched, but also quiet. It made me feel more aware than ever of the deep chasm between these men and me. I was alone again, shut inside my tent, too early in the long, claustrophobic night, in order to escape from the insects that filled the air. The others had come together with all the naturalness of men in a dark place, warmed and comforted by a fire, while I had rejected their fellowship and walked away into the night. I could tell myself I had been irritated by the juvenile way they were talking, but the deeper and more vexing thing inside me was plainly there and I could not deny it, a natural shunning of what was normal and pleasant in the company of others, leaving me like an old dog nursing a wound, licking, jealous, with its own tongue.

I lay down and waited to be taken away into unconsciousness, welcoming the fatigue, numbing like an opiate now that it had finished drubbing my limbs, that would drag me down into the dark.

In the end sleep came quickly but it did not last. Noise and static and odd burst of southern Baptist drawl beat their way into my consciousness. I sat up, confused for a moment and then awake. Someone was playing with a radio in the dark. The cloud of biting insects that had gathered in the windless night air must have driven the others to hide inside their tents soon after I had. Daniel had pitched his tent right alongside my own and that was why the noise seemed so loud and close. As soon he was inside he must have switched his radio on and started twiddling the knob from sermon to sermon on the American sponsored evangelical channels that were all you could ever find in the darkness of the African night. None of the stations seemed to be what he wanted. He held on to each one for the length of half a preacher's sentence and then twisted the knob on to the next channel, so there was not even the restfulness of a single uninterrupted stream of sound forming itself into a single voice with a single story to tell.

The jumble of amplified noise exploded through the thin canvas walls of the tent, shredding the stillness of the night with half-caught phrases that coalesced into a comfortless announcement of the fires of hell and the power of God's chosen.

For a few unresolved minutes I lay in my sweat, awake and furious, but restraining myself, waiting to see if Daniel would give up and knowing that he would not. Daniel was an insomniac. I imagined him, lonely and already beginning to flip after too long a stint in the field. The U.N. was like that. The bosses, white, Asian or African, lived and worked in Nairobi, but the Kenyans they recruited were doomed to spend their lives on over-extended tours of duty in the field, desperate to get one of the rare, almost mythical postings back in the capital, where they would be able to live with their families while still benefiting from the big U.N. pay cheques. It did this to them in the end, addling their minds with sheer loneliness and homesickness, so that they could not sleep at night but ended up like Daniel now, surfing the airwaves for some voice of comfort and finding only the heavy accents from the American Midwest endlessly preaching the end of all things.

I switched on my torch and lay for five minutes or so watching the second hand on my watch go round. Then I snapped. I just wanted the noise, the grizzly, self-satisfied American preaching, to stop. It was like an infectious disease, spreading the lonely, half-mad insomnia through the darkness, destroying all the comforts I had designed and ritualised to stave it off, like the bare concrete wall of a prison cell finally bursting through the illusory covering of wallpaper and pictures that have been hung to cover the comfortless dreary reality that is that really waited for you. I raised myself and with a vicious tone in my voice that I had not expected, I shouted out as loud as I could: 'Turn that bloody row off!'

I heard the click of the radio switch. Then there was the silence I needed. No other sound.

In the morning Daniel was surly at breakfast. I ignored it. We were not part of the same team. There was no need to mend fences or struggle to get on. Fuck him.

But, even as I formed these thoughts, I knew it was just a pose and the words would not rescue me. The sleepless nights were my own inner hell, the endless churning through the memories that would not leave me or comfort me, but only brought on more strongly the knowledge of my own lack of self-belief. Inside I could feel a deal of sympathy, but I had let the other side, the grumpy old white man, come through and painted myself even further into the caricature I already knew I had become in the minds of the others.

I slurped down a cup of instant coffee and ate some of the cheese crackers that were all I ever wanted for breakfast here. The only alternative was the uji-like porridge the women cooked up for the others. Then I got down to sorting out my kit, especially the emergency items that I intended to take with me on the drive.

My mind was not clear. The woman and the child had come to me again during the night, clearer than before. I could not remember what they had said, but it had troubled me. I had woken up with strange, childish tears running down my cheeks. There had been something I should have done, but I could not remember what it was, only that it was important. We had been in Egypt, climbing Mt Sinai on a hot, bright morning. The child had made it all the way up the endless steps but had needed to be carried down on the back of a camel by one of the Bedou touts who lined the dusty road down. It had been a special day, a birthday I thought, and the air had been crisp and sharp as never before. I had been happy, happier than I could remember. We were laughing. She had said something, but I could not remember the words, just as I could not remember the sound of her voice except in the dreams. Now the images came again in blurred half memories, interfering with my concentration as I laid the items out on my camp bed and rummaged in my rucksack for new batteries for the torch.

There was an excitement inside me that kept out the dark and anticipated the arrival of Father Severino in his landcruiser. It was not just the trip, but something more, something about the man himself and the thought that we would meet and talk and the sure knowledge that our talk would take us far beyond the desultory exchanges that were all I ever managed with my colleagues or with Simon.

The best part of the day went by before I heard the rumbling of the priest's Landcruiser coming down the hill and in a way I was glad of this delay. The enthusiasm that had been kindled within me was accompanied by a kind of shyness that made me wary of our next meeting.

Simon's behaviour was part of it too. He was smiling more than ever before, as though he knew something and found it amusing.

We spent the day seated around a large table under the generous spread of branches of the ficus tree that dominated the compound, pretending to complete the WFP table and in order to do this making the conversion table from livelihoods and food shortages to nutritional requirements. Simon was adept at massaging the figures. He had worked out that by claiming a failure of the unmonitored lesser rains that fell in the first part of the year he would have a basis on which the relative poverty and food-aid dependency of the community could be justified and he worked it into every line of the chart that was slowly filling on the rough table top under the tree. He faced his three visitors across the table, alternating between an aggressively upright pose and an indolent slouch, and answered our questions with his smile.

And yet it was not as if Simon mattered so very much in the end. In any case, I could not really resent his behaviour. It was what they did. Wasn't this their country, anyway, their toic, their swamp, their war? And who could ever blame them for trying to milk the aid machine as best they could, or blame their leaders for trying to build the bases of their power on the only economic input that there was, the food drops, guaranteed as long as they could demonstrate the prevalence of poverty and need? It was not my role to trash all that. In the end, I had no role in this drama. I was just a minor nuisance and the tolerance of the tall, black men around me was no different from their tolerance of the mosquitoes in the night air. I knew this is my inner being, even if the words to confirm it might never be spoken.

What chewed up and shredded my intestines, however, as I sat in the sweaty, fetid shade, pretending to be indifferent to the passing minutes and hours, was the certain knowledge that I was going to meet someone who defined his role out here in a way that did not fit the paradigm and that, cliché though it might seem or, in fact, be, I would have no option but to enter into a particular kind of relationship with the man I would inevitably call 'Father', even though I could already guess from appearances that he was far younger than me. And the real hard fact underneath it all, when you stripped it down and got to what was really there inside, was how did you speak to someone so full of hope and action, someone who was doing all the things he did with his own bare hands so as to demonstrate what he would call the love of God and someone else, more modern or less controversial, perhaps, would call basic humanity? The question was still the same, whatever you called him, how did you approach him, what did you say to this positively good man, when you so much wanted to be his friend, to somehow draw strength from whatever it was that he saw in fallen humanity and all its foibles and the great and unbearable evils into which it fell? How did you approach him, this person, strong or naïve, whatever he was, who, unlike you, did not wake up every morning with a curse in the very taste of the saliva in his mouth, who did not wish God, if he existed at all, might rip the entrails out of your belly, rip your flesh apart in any way he chose, do whatever he wanted so long as it would stop the dreams from coming, stop the memories, just switch off the images that tormented you, with no promise of eternity, just the peace of an endless dark sleep, just the switch going off and a deep slow sigh escaping from your breast into the air. How did you speak to this person who was all about light when you were all darkness within?

In the end it seemed you just walked down to the Catholic church compound, knocked on the door and said 'hello'.

The compound had a high wooden fence around it with gates made out of corrugated iron sheets. The watchman let me in without any questions, pointing to the small wooden house in one corner across the yard. A large, dust-covered four-wheel drive Toyota Landcruiser of the old-fashioned long wheelbase kind was parked next to it under a rough wood and canvas shade. Along the side of the house there were a few tired looking plants in pots under the shade of a small tree, some kind of ficus. In the Ethiopian Highlands in the old time I would have now what tree it was, but here I knew nothing. That was part of the sham and posturing of these expeditions to the field, they did not amount to much and ended in the thirty seconds of a bumpy take-off and the flight back to the never-never land of Loki and the other world of Nairobi beyond. By contrast, the vehicle looked worn and used and in need of cleaning. It spoke of permanence here in the wild lands, no quick in and out, but the long hard slog of a daily grind through the heat and dirt and unchanging lack of everything that elsewhere could be taken for granted. A mother hen strutted across the space in from of the small porch at the front of the house, followed by her chicks in a tight group. I walked slowly over, not wanting to alarm them or accidentally tread on one of the small, cheeping balls of fluff. No-one answered my knock on the half-open door, so I stepped inside.

The room I entered was dark and sparsely furnished with a wooden table and rudimentary chairs of the kind they made in small workshops anywhere in Africa. There was nobody there and I did not want to go further into the interior uninvited. I called out 'Hello'. My voice sounded curiously detached from the rest of me, thin and insecure. There was no response. I stayed still, observing myself, wondering what the person I was watching would do next. I might sit down, or, better, I should go back outside into the sunlight.

I had turned round and was about go back over towards the door, when I heard the shuffling noise of someone approaching wearing plastic flip-flops and I turned back to see Sister Lucy enter the room from the short, dark corridor that led to the rooms at the back. 'Hello,' she said, speaking quietly but clearly, like a nurse in a hospital ward, 'I hope you have not waited long. It has been a long day and the Father is resting.'

'No, not at all,' I replied. 'I had just arrived. I hope I did not disturb you.' My words felt stiff and formal and I was aware of feeling awkward, like an unexpected intruder who does not know whether he has come at the right time.

She smiled briefly and then said 'I am going to make tea. Will you have a cup with us?' Her voice was flat, so that I could not tell whether I was supposed to accept this invitation or not. In the end I thanked her with the same formal stiffness and sat down at the table uninvited.

'The Father will be with us soon,' she added.

On the table in front of me she set a large tin mug half full of steaming tea with the milk and probably, I guessed, sugar already added. I raised it to my lips and burnt them on the hot metal. I flinched and let out an involuntary yelp that coincided with the priest's arrival in the room.

'What was that? Are you OK?' Father Severino came immediately over to where I was sitting.

"Yes, I'm fine. Just a hot mug. I'm sorry to disturb you, Father. I came too early." I stood and held my hand out.

In the quiet shadows of the kitchen Father Severino looked younger that he had done in the sunlight. His skin had a dark, Latin hue. His hair was thick and black. His eyes were dark and soft under thick black eyebrows. By contrast on his unshaven chin he had the patchy stubble that signalled a high proportion of indigenous blood in his veins. His chest, arms and shoulders were powerful, like those of a body builder or a man who was used to heavy physical work.

The more I looked at him close up now, the more the image formed itself in my mind of an archetype, almost a caricature, of the Latin American revolutionary, or more probably the liberation theologian, something that could only have been spawned by the unique and bitter stew of Spanish colonial history. It was Graham Greene, not Charles Dickens: Catholicism, racism, the Monroe doctrine, massacred tribes and endless shanty towns, stuff that I found hard to wholly believe in, because it had no parallel template in my own background. It had something fundamental in it that was born out of the Counter-reformation, a visceral love for the poor, perhaps, but one that rushed straight from the Middle Ages to Marxism without pausing to take in the harsh, alienating disciplines of Adam Smith or Malthus or Bentham. It was a skin I could not myself put on.

The priest smiled as he had done the previous day. It was a good smile, like hospitality itself, kind and open. 'So you came for your "tea-time"?' he said with a slight question in his tone.

'Yes, Father. I came, but it seems I have already burnt my lips on the tea cup.' His eyes began to show concern again, so I added, quickly and dismissively, 'It's nothing. Just trying to make another little joke. Not really very funny.'

Father Severino sat down, gesturing to me to do the same with a quick movement of his hand. 'I am glad you came,' he said. 'I wanted to talk to you.'

The questions that were burning to be unleashed inside my mind were all about the day that was to come, about the track into the dry bush, the vehicle and the Jiye tribe waiting at the other end. I wanted the next hours to be behind us already. I felt insecure, sure somehow that Simon would find some way of preventing our departure, some SRRC regulation, some order from the commander of the camp on the hill. I would not feel calm or good inside, I knew, until we were on the road and Simon's office and compound were lost in the red dust thrown up behind us, for Simon loomed in my mind now like an evil spirit bent on keeping me trapped in this small, illusory world where nothing true could ever be seen or found. All the same, I knew I had to control this nervousness. It was childish and it was undisciplined. I did not yet have the guarantee I wanted that the journey would for sure take place. The priest might change his mind or decide his vehicle was not up to the trip. I had been in these situations on many occasions. The passenger, which was what I was or would be, had no power over when or whether at all a journey he had set out to make would go ahead and experience had taught me that the only way to cope with the disappointment of cancellation was not to raise your inner expectations too soon or too high.

It was a game really. I would show a larger than expected interest in the work of the church. I would show a larger than expected interest in the work of the priest here in Boma - hang onto his every word and ask questions. This would, in any case, be useful. I needed his knowledge to help me, subjectively at least, re-evaluate the information Simon had been channelling into the tables that we had spent our time completing. Only after covering all of that would I broach the subject of the next day's journey, subtly and without an excess of enthusiasm, since that had always seemed to usher in a negative outcome on past occasions, as though the enthusiasm itself could bring bad luck or, more likely, act in some destructive way on the good-will of the other.

'Father, tell me about what you do here,' I said.

But the priest did not respond the way I had expected him to. 'You saw that yesterday,' he said. 'First I want to know about you. I know nothing and I know it is interesting – what you do. And in fact,' he smiled up at Sister Lucy and took the mug of tea which she was holding out to him, 'you have not even told me your name.'

Before I could respond, the priest took a large slurping gulp of his tea and then added 'Besides, you will see more of our work tomorrow when we go to the Jiye. There you will see people who really have nothing, who really need your help.'

I could not keep from smiling at this. The excitement I had felt the day before and throughout this day so far had come to life in my chest, accelerating the rhythm of my breathing. I felt I was being drawn into a conspiracy - a conspiracy of the good. The thing I chased and always found to be illusory, which I had always taken to be the need for a sense of purpose in what I was supposed to be doing, had after all reared itself up out of nothing, just a few words spoken over the rim of a scalding hot tea mug. And I knew now that tomorrow I would carry a responsibility with me. I would observe and record and would translate what I found into a humanitarian assessment report. I'd submit it to the coordination office and, inevitably, that would lead to action of some kind, my own little action, my little band of hitherto neglected villages from a forgotten tribe.

It was like finding a lost faith, breeding enthusiasm as it grew again. I would tell the others to come too. I could use their skills, especially the nutritionist, Samuel. This would be like what they were meant to be doing in the first place on this mission and it would bring a return to sanity and meaningfulness.

Father Severino's voice stirred me out of this inner dialogue. 'I need to fix the vehicle first, though,' he said. 'We will set off immediately after I have said mass tomorrow – it is Sunday, you know. The truck must be in good shape. The brakes are worn out. Coming down the hill destroys them. I will change the brake pads.'

When I heard this it was clear to me at once that, however trivial it might seem, making or failing to make the repair was the issue on which success depended. I stood up quickly. 'It'll be dark soon, Father. I'd better go so you can get on.'

'Why not help me?'

I had not expected this invitation. Practical men usually just got on with things and expected others to keep out of the way. It was a way of declaring their superior status in an undefined but instinctively understood male hierarchy.

'I'm probably not much use,' I said. 'You know, I've always wanted to be better at fixing things, especially vehicles, but I never got round to it. So I doubt I'd be much help to you.'

'Well, let's go.' Father Severino totally ignored this remark and was already talking down a blue overall from a hook behind the door and pulling it over his clothes. 'I'm afraid I don't have one of these for you.'

'An overall? Never mind, I'm not dressed up.'

'"Overall", that's right. "Overall".' Father Severino smiled again as he said this, as though discovering or recovering the English expression were a point of great satisfaction to him. Without saying more we both got up from the table and went out into the yard.

Outside the sun was already low over the fence. I reckoned we would have an hour before it got dark. 'Luckily, it is only the front brakes. I did the rear ones last week,' he said as we crossed the yard.

For the next two hours we worked hard. I did what Father Severino told me, like an apprentice in a workshop. I liked it. I liked the smell of grease and diesel fumes and the grime that smeared itself into the cracked skin of my fingers. It made me feel practical, male and whole.

When we had finished the job, we washed our hands in paraffin before heading back to the house in the twilight gloom of the sudden African night.

'Where did you learn this, Father?' I asked.

'My brother is a mechanic in Zacatecas. I would have been the same. My family were poor. But I was the clever one in the family, the one who read books and liked to go to school. My brothers preferred to earn a few pesos shining shoes. And so one day the Jesuits found me, or I prefer to think Our Lord Jesus Christ found me.' He said this last without any trace of affectedness. It was natural, it was what he believed and felt and lived and it made him whole in a way few from the modern world would know or feel. It reached directly across centuries into the swamps of the vast emptiness, into the hearts of the tall, thin, dark people who lived here with their cattle, it was the way they thought and felt, directly at one with the sky and water and grasslands that were their life and the stuff of the gods they knew and which shaped, made and destroyed their lives.

'I wish I was practical,' I said, letting the thoughts in my mind become words on my lips without stopping to interrogate them. It seemed quite natural to do this here with Father Severino. 'I mean,' I continued, 'So that I could spend whole days just fixing things without having to think or write stupid reports or go to meetings that decide nothing. Just fix things – engines, machines, vehicles – and see them working at the end and know that I knew how to keep them running and if anything went wrong anywhere I'd be able to fix them.' I was muttering the words to myself, as though I did not really want to share them.

'What did you say?' Father Severino asked, as anyone would have done, and I was obliged to clarify.

'I was just thinking it would be good to be practical, like you are. I mean it would be very useful out here. I have been thinking that since yesterday when we met you welding the girders for the church roof.'

It was true, I knew, since I knew myself better than anyone, and I had long given up denying the things I saw in myself. There had been no elder brother who was a mechanic in my family. In my home nobody ever did anything practical, like car maintenance or woodwork or home plumbing, just as nobody did any of the more exotic sports – sailing or fishing – that required equipment. It was a closed world with the feel of a members-only club which I was barred from entering. As an adult I had picked up bits and pieces here and there, but I knew I did not belong. If you did not enter young enough to pass through the various rituals of initiation, you could never belong to that world.

'Well it's useful, I suppose,' he said. 'But a lot of people can do those things. It is not something special, not a gift.' His words were reassuring, as though by speaking of gifts and disassociating the practical world from those special things, he had reduced its power to intimidate. 'You can learn everything like that. If you wish, I can teach you to weld. It will surprise you how easy it is. In fact, safety is the main issue. That is why I have not taught others here. Not yet. One day we will have a vocational school. One day....' He sighed, as though the immensity of the effort that lay between the here and now and the attainment of the dream was sucking the energy right out of him as he spoke.

'You are tired, Father, I'll let you rest. I'm glad I was able to help. Tomorrow will be good. It will make all the difference to our mission.' I found myself saying this with a warmth that I would have preferred to suppress, a gush of enthusiasm that came out before I could tie it down, increasing the discomfort of a stilted conversation that part of me wanted to see develop into something long and profound, a discussion on the margins of personal experience that would externalise the restless closed-circuit failures to make sense of anything I did that kept me awake at night.

'Wait, though,' Father Severino reached out and gently caught my sleeve. 'You are very strange, my friend. You still do not tell me your name? Do you even have a name? Do you hide it? Why do you hide it?' He leaned forward bringing his face closer. In the shadows his eyes were black holes.

'I don't hide it,' I said. For a moment I felt the warmth and the enthusiasm of a moment before hover on the edge of something wholly different, a stab of anger and a sinking of my spirits away from the heights, at the thought that anyone might have thought I should want to do something as crass as to hide my name from others.

The moment passed and I could sense my voice becoming measured and without emotion again. 'We lost the thread back there, Father. Then we started working. I have a name, of course I do, like everybody else. Just like you. If you want to know, my name is Richards.'

'Just Richards?' he asked, inevitably. Then he added 'Well, Richards. I am pleased to meet you.' He held out his hand in grace gesture that might have been mockery. I could not tell.

We shook hands and as we did so I could feel the distaste that came whenever I spoke too much after drinking a beer too many in uncertain company, the opening of doors I had long promised to myself that I would keep shut – not that so much could ever be tied up in the revelation of a name.

Obviously not - and yet it was as though one thing had already indicated its intention of leading to another, from initial familiarity to something far less savoury, a wallowing revelation of the things, the pictures and the unshaped misery of a landscape of the soul that from time to time took of forms and became articulate, though usually in carefully arranged solitude.

I remained silent as we entered the house, but I noticed Sister Lucy had already laid the table for three and I knew it would be churlish now to take my leave without first sharing a meal. I was also aware that the unappetising stews I had been eating with the others had allowed a powerful hunger to build up inside me over the last few days. The smell of meat and vegetables coming from the pot was bubbling on top of the gas ring was good.

# 4.

*Saturday night continued*

The beef and vegetable stew that Sister Lucy ladled over a mound of rice on my plate looked and smelled good. I knew it was the same simple stuff I had been eating at the compound, but it looked and smelled better. I shovelled some rice soaked in the stew onto my spoon and was starting to chew it when I looked up and saw that she was looking at me with a look of intense disapproval in her eye. I stopped and put the spoon down in the dish.

Father Severino said a brief grace in English. Then he in turn looked up, smiled and said 'Tonight I think we should drink some wine, Sister Lucy, in honour of our guest. We have one bottle, which I brought with me from Nairobi, so let's open it. It will only go bad if we keep it in the bottle. Nothing lasts long in this climate.'

He opened the cupboard behind his head and pulled out a bottle of Chilean Merlot of the sort they sold in the supermarkets in Westlands. He uncorked it and then served the wine in the glass beakers that Sister Lucy had intended for water when she laid the table. 'We can drink water later,' he said. 'Now a toast. What should we toast? You decide, Richards.'

I thought about it for a moment. It would have been easy enough just to suggest something fatuous and inconsequential, but that would not have fitted what he was asking for. In the end I replied with what was most on my mind. 'To tomorrow, to a successful day…'

'Yes, that's right!' he said with an enthusiasm that would normally have irritated me, but which I accepted now as a manifestation of something genuine in the man - honesty or integrity, or perhaps some kind of naivety. That seemed appropriate for a mission priest. 'To a successful day and to a safe return.'

'Amen,' said Sister Lucy and put her glass down after taking a sip so small it hardly would have counted in places where people really drank. She looked at me briefly and I could feel the challenge in her eye, as though she found the bottle of wine sinful in itself and blamed my presence in the house for its presence open on the table before us, the evil genie it contained now out and seeking to make mischief.

'I promise you will be fascinated by the Jiye, Richards. They are simple, good people and there are in need of your help.' Father Severino spoke with a passion that stopped his words from sounding condescending. He took a large sip of wine, greedy with the need to lubricate the flow of his enthusiasm. 'They have nothing. They have lost everything they had. We done what we can, but it is little. We have dug a well and put a pump. I persuaded the SRRC to do that with the drill rig they keep in Rumbek. Simon was very helpful. He made them get the Buffalo to fly it down here.'

'Simon?'

'Yes, of course.' Father Severino said this with slow emphasis. 'He can be very helpful if he sees the purpose in something.'

I could have reacted to this with some snide comment about the real purpose being the broadening of Simon's own power base, but it would have been out of place and might have spoilt the evening. I knew that without any effort of the mind. This was not a time for the cynical games into which conversations about this big, sad country and the aid business, which was the only business it supported, usually slipped. I did not have to change anything fundamentally about the way

I thought or the things I saw and had seen. They were not relevant. I had to build a bridge and cross over it in order to secure the future. The journey that had now become so nearly certain had taken on an importance that was on the brink of being mystical, containing a solution to the questions that had appeared to be without answer. I had a vehicle and I had a guide.

'Tell me about your work here, Father,' I said. 'I mean, how did you come to be here? It seems so far from Mexico.'

'I am not the only Mexican in Africa,' he said with a slight laugh. 'In our order there are many: priests and sisters. The order has members from all over the world. You know that the Church is universal. So many come to work in Africa, if it is their calling. For me it was my calling.' He refilled his glass, smiling in response to Sister Lucy's sharp glance.

'But did you always want to come to Sudan? I mean did you choose it?'

'We do not choose. It is calling. This was mine.'

'And you came here, to this place, to Boma, alone?'

'With Sister Lucy, of course.'

There was a certainty in the priest's responses to my questions that could easily have led me to believe we were talking at cross purposes. But we were not. I was sure of that.

The night had come now outside the window and the air was full of the trilling of crickets and the two-stroke staccato of the frogs. Father Severino looked across at me in silence for a moment, listening to the sounds of the night. Then he spoke again, his voice quieter, graver. 'We have been here six months now. You saw the school and the new church we are building. There is also a farm. It's like a vegetable garden really. We are teaching the community to grow more vegetables. But there is too much to do. And there are many things I do not know. We need help. The people have so little…'

There was for the first time a hint of despair in the way he allowed this last sentence to tail off, as though fatigue and loneliness in the face of the vast, shapeless emptiness that stretched forever out across the water-logged plain could sometimes rise up and challenge the firmest of convictions, puncturing hope with arrows drawn from the empty darkness that I had come to know only too well, the stuff of my sleepless nights. The priest was young and strong and most of the time it seemed he knew where he was going. But the emptiness was patient and was always waiting.

I wanted to reach out across the crack that I could see opening up in the smooth plain wall of conviction. When you both faced that big emptiness, you ended up knowing that you shared some common ground. 'I think what you are doing here is good,' I said, 'better than anything else I have seen. Most of our projects are just bits and pieces. We fly in, we fly out. We don't stay, we don't know the people in these places. We just call them beneficiaries and turn them into numbers in our reports. Sometimes I feel I come on trips like this just so I won't forget what they look like. But I'll never get to know them or understand their world from the inside. Not like you. You are here to stay.'

Now that I had started, the thoughts and feelings flowed into my mind with a coherence that they lacked when I was lying awake at night flipping through the pages of a mental diary that had ultimately become confused to the point of senselessness. 'Let me tell you, Father,' I said, taking a swig of the wine in my glass, 'about the way it is with us. I'm not saying we do no good at all or that no lives are saved, just that it does not work the way it should, it does not leave you feeling good. It's almost as if the good things come by accident.'

The priest was looking at me intensely now as I spoke, but with the same gentle darkness in his eyes. Sister Lucy stood up and served more of the stew and more rice to both of us. I noticed the way she looked at Father Severino as she served him. There was a great tenderness in that look, the admiration women sometimes show for priests and never for other men, a mixture of devotion, as to a saint or to a master, and something altogether more physical, a maternal instinct that must come from the sure knowledge that the priest was a man who lived alone without a wife to comfort or support him. And what was essentially physical, or instinctive, could so easily shift into something else. I caught myself wondering for an instant about the relationship between these two people, a man and woman living together in a place like this, sharing a burden. It would only be natural, after all, if they were to be something more than the priest and nun in the house they shared.

I felt her eye on me as she stood there. I knew that she was asking with her eyes whether I wanted more of the stew, but it felt as though she had read my thoughts and it brought on a sudden dirty-minded school-boy shame. My eyes lowered involuntarily to the table and then rolled sideways up again, this time to look at the priest, who was sitting calmly, chewing his food and waiting for me to continue. His patience began to feel like the patience of the confessional and, whatever my earlier intentions might have been and whatever the rule book I might have claimed to have made for myself might say, I found myself already on the point of talking about the inner thoughts and troublesome memories that caused me to hate myself whenever through too much drinking or too much being alone I let my guard down with other men. I had been that way on just a few occasions after drinking one beer too many in an ex-pat bar in Westlands or one of the camps at Loki, and I had always hated myself afterwards. Here and now, however, it seemed as though these thoughts could be shared without shame.

'Let me tell you about my first experience in the field here in Sudan, Father,' I said, 'just to give you an idea of what this great big operation is like when you strip it down. That time there were reports of a large displacement of Dinka villagers in Western Upper Nile after some sort of activity by pro-government Nuer militias. The daily Operation Lifeline Sudan meeting decided that the head of Unicef should go and take a look and I might as well go with him, since both of us were new. The plan was for us to stay at the Unicef camp Nyal.

'I can remember the feeling I had about it all. It was like a huge military machine. You had to have all the documents to start with before you could even leave Nairobi – Sudan Government visa, combined SPLM and SRRA permit, combined SPDF and RASS permit, OLS survival instruction booklet and the special kit with things like guinea worm filters in it. Nobody seems to take those kits that seriously out here, except for myself. I suppose there must be a frustrated boy-scout inside me,' I looked over at the priest, inviting him with my eyes to laugh or grin at this, but Father Severino did not react. He continued to sit, still and attentive, eating slowly, inviting me with his attention and his silence to continue. So I did.

'That first time I saw Wilson Airport in the evening I felt like I was stepping into one of the drawings in a Tintin book. I remember looking at the line of nineteen-thirties aircraft hangars and small propeller-driven planes, Caravans for the most part, together with the odd Dakota - they still use them with revamped engines – and thinking it was like one of those pictures from the past you sometimes see in travel agencies…

'We flew up the Rift Valley in the twilight. When we got there Loki was different from anywhere else I had ever been to. I expect you know it yourself. You must have been there, stayed there on your way up here. The camps with security guards at the gate and barbed wire around them, rows of four-wheel drive vehicles with UN and NGO logos on their doors, parked outside low, prefab buildings. And the local people, Turkanas, almost naked with their skinny sickly children around them, squatting in the dust outside the gates and watching the vehicles go in and out.

'That first time it felt nameless and dangerous in the middle of the desert. The UN security team were all ex 'Special Forces', the sort of people who let you know they're tough. They run around in uniforms shouting and they carry walkie-talkie radios that suddenly spit out distorted electronic messages. Everything they do seems fuelled by adrenalin and it makes you feel small and civilian and somehow ill-equipped for the place you are going to up ahead, north across the desert, over the unseen border. They briefed us in a room full of maps and camping equipment with the radio crackling all the time in the background. They made it seem as though we were taking big risks. It all makes you feel special. I have to admit it did that to me. I was caught up in it all. I was excited and self-important.

'I don't want to make too long a story of it now, Father. You know this place better that I ever will. So I'll spare you the details of the flight. It is pretty amazing though, looking down on all that emptiness, seeing the brown turn to green as you reach the swamps. Every time I do it I find my eyes following the cattle trails you can see, wondering about the people down there, what they're doing, what they're thinking. But you never see any actual people. Too high up, I guess.

'Anyway, the camp at Nyal is right on the edge of the swamp. At night we sat outside in a cloud of insects and were eaten alive, more so than there, much more. And in the morning I heard the children singing for the first time. I remember thinking their voices were like angels, Father.' I paused again, expecting a comment on this, but Father Severino simply nodded very slightly to indicate that I should continue.

'We flew to see the displaced villagers in an area near some sort of front line. From the air it was impossible to distinguish IDPs from pastoralists moving from one place to the next with their cattle, the way they do. On the ground it was chaotic. The pilot was nervous, so we had to move fast with limited time. I can see it like a photograph. There was a big cattle camp. We had to walk close by the big hump-backed bulls. Some NGO had already drilled a well, but it was too near an SPLA camp and the soldiers had taken it over.

'And then what did we find, out there in the middle of all this confusion? We found a small tent with a Medecins Sans Frontieres flag at the entrance and a line of people waiting to be inoculated by a doctor – a woman, French and very elegant. I cannot remember her exactly, but I am sure she was wearing one those chiffon scarves, like a caricature – I remember thinking that at the time. She didn't seem aware... Anyway, the point is I could not work out what was going on and nobody was saying anything that made sense. There seemed to be the same confusion on the ground as in the air when we tried to work out the difference between people displaced by fighting and people on the move anyway, just moving their cattle around, the way they do, according to the seasons.

'We flew back to the camp at Nyal and then used up the rest of the day, like a bunch of tourists, going for a spin across the swamp through the reed beds on one of the Unicef's two fan-driven swamp buggies. Apparently they were imported at some enormous cost and then they suddenly realised you are not allowed to deliver petrol by air, so they couldn't get any fuel for them. Do you know what they did to solve that? Can you believe it, they converted the engines to diesel! They contracted a pair of specialist mechanics from Florida and flew them out specially to do the job. They turned out to be a rough pair of rednecks who got into trouble with the Kenyan immigration police. I was told it was for trying to smuggle a gun in so they could do some hunting, but it could have been anything. The war and its rules didn't mean anything to them. When we were there the Unicef people told me the machines have never worked properly and have never been repaired. That's not the story you read in their glossy brochures...'

I had to pause in order to breath properly and take stock. The words were spinning out as fast as the stockpile of angry images and thoughts could make them. The soft dark eyes of the priest were still on me; the expression on his face was calm, receptive. This was what priests were trained to do, of course. It was their job to listen until the words dried up and there was a space left behind where they had been. In the end the space was always what interested them, not the words. They would just come out and be lost and all the things you thought really mattered would turn out to be no cleverer than any other idea you had ever had or word that you had spoken.

'So that is it, Father, my first impression,' I said. 'Just confusion, stupid, messy confusion. WFP delivers food left, right and centre according to its own logic, a huge crowd of NGOs do bits and pieces here and there, and we deal with the small political storms and crises, usually to do with humanitarian policy or the endless peace process. The big political issues bring a whole crowd of self-important old men swarming in from around the globe…

I looked into his eyes across the table, expecting some reaction from him at this point, now that my anger was plain for him to see. 'Do you want me to continue?' I asked and I took his silence to be an affirmative. So I went on. 'Let me tell you about my latest trip – up to Mabaan County, where there had never been an intervention before. We had reports of people suffering badly in the IDP camps up there, the ones displaced by the oil exploration in Eastern Upper Nile out of Malakal – no, I mean further north, downstream. I took a team there. While we were doing it, it felt fantastic. We walked away twenty miles between the two main villages, we saw everything we could, held meetings with the villages, camped in one of their compounds and ate the pig they slaughtered for us.

'By the way, Father, did you know they are the only tribe I have heard of in the Nile valley or the Horn of Africa who keep pigs? They have them running around everywhere throughout the village, eating whatever scraps they can and looking fat and healthy, while the village dogs are scrawny and half-starved and just lie there looking miserable.

'Anyway, we saw that the main problem they had was just that. The pigs run around everywhere and share the few water points with the people. The people are too crowded together, since they have been displaced from their villages and they're living together now in these enormous informal settlements. And none of them has ever dug a pit latrine or had any hygiene training. They just go in the bush. The kids die because of that, nothing else, dysentery kills them. We wrote a report saying they needed some wells drilled and a mass of hygiene education. And what happened? They got a WFP food drop.'

I stopped talking, even though there could have been so much more to tell. I suppose I was exhausted by the flow of my own rhetoric. It had been like making a speech, a pointless, wholly negative speech that I had rehearsed too often inside my head and I found myself wishing I had kept quiet, or else just talked about the good things. I knew there were plenty. The waste and the futility seemed pasted onto the inside of my own mind, part of my own perception that I now felt ashamed of sharing. I looked across at Father Severino again, expecting that now there would be some reaction, a refutation of my jaundiced view that weighed so heavily on me that it must be wrong and must demand and receive an answer from the messenger of hope and light. But the priest seemed only to be listening, still eating and watching me with infinite patience.

'Do you want me to say more?' I asked for what seemed like the hundredth time. 'I could go on. Let's talk about development, about the schools that are needed, like the one you have built. After all, it is only a matter of time, maybe only months, before they have peace here and then they are supposed to get the peace dividend. You can see the leaders already counting the Mercedes they will buy for themselves once the aid money really starts to pour in. Even Simon must be counting on getting something for himself. The donors are lining up with their programmes – good governance, education, roads, you name it. But all it means is that they will end up in the hands of the economists. Once development start it all becomes economics and, whatever fancy jargon they use nowadays, all the bullshit about pro-poor growth and empowering the poor, in the end they only have one model and that is transformation – you know, turning agricultural backwaters into something like England in the industrial revolution – and their mantra is growth: growth, growth,

growth. People are just numbers and large populations mean large pools of cheap labour. Nobody cares about the shitty, wasted lives; the model moves on and eventually things are supposed to get better – only they never quite do, because they never quite catch up with where they need to be. That's your lot's fault in part, you know - population growth. Every day there's more babies to feed. We're pretty good at keeping them all alive nowadays, but we're keeping them alive so that they can live in shanty towns. Can you tell me why that is, Father? Why the model can only deliver its promise by turning people into numbers and condemning then to a life like that?'

Without my noticing my voice had risen as I spoke these final words. I was not drunk, but the wine had been enough to open the door progressively to a point where I was making a damned speech, saying the things I sometimes thought when the darkness was on me and challenging the world and the man who was sitting on the other side of the table to give an answer. I half expected the priest to continue to sit in studious, provocative silence and for the sake of what remained of my self-respect was therefore preparing myself – belatedly - to do the same, to wait either for the other to reply or for the high charge of my rhetoric to cool itself down to the level of normal intercourse and then to fade into inconsequence.

Father Severino reached forward with the bottle and refilled his glass. I looked up to say thank you, but before the words had left my lips he began, at long last, to speak very quietly. 'I know how you feel,' he said. 'I have the same doubts at times. Does that surprise you?'

The dark, empty eyes were on me across the table, gentle and passive-seeming, like his voice, a depth that sought me out and asked me to share the questions and whatever else there was in the darkness of the night and of our minds.

'I have wondered at times,' he continued, 'why God allows so much suffering to go on in this world. Believe me, I know about it and not just from this small work I do with Sister Lucy here. My own family were poor, you know. My father lost his job and went to the Unites States as a bracero. Then his health stopped him from going and for a time we had nothing, no money coming in to support us – and I was the second son in a family of seven children. There were times when we had nothing to eat except a few stale tortillas. My youngest sister used to crawl into the choza we lived in. many times we would go to school with no food in our stomachs. Do you know how it feels to walk a long way to school when you are hungry and then to have nothing to eat at all until you walk home again at the end of your lessons? It is terrible feeling, something that no child should have to feel. And sometimes some of us would be kicked out of class by the teacher because our clothes were old and ragged. They said we were dirty and it was disrespectful to come to school like that. The other children, the ones who had new uniforms and smart white shoes, used to laugh at us and call us things – stupid things that I do not remember. But they hurt when we were children.

'The worst day was when my mother miscarried with her eighth baby. She gave birth at home, like she always did. She suffered terribly. I still remember the way she cried. We thought she was going to die, but it was the baby who was born dead. They buried her in a shoe box because we could not afford a coffin. I still remember her, the little sister I never had.'

He said all this in the same quiet, gentle voice he had been speaking in all evening, without any melodrama or emotional colouring, but with the same warmth that had been so disarming from the start. Then he went on: 'So I too have been bitter, Richards. I have cursed God, the way so many other people have done, although I have not cursed the ones who give to the poor with their programmes in quite the way you have. But then I was fortunate, as I told you. I like to read and that was what saved me. At first it was a way to escape from the terrible world I seemed to be condemned to live in, but then it took me to the school run by the fathers, were I was educated. And from there I went into the seminary. I learnt many things, but above all I learnt to think and to reflect and to pray. I came to see that the world is a paradoxical place, because it is a fallen world and were are fallen people. And I knew from the beginning, as surely as I knew I had been found by our Lord, that I would want to follow his way in the work I would do. I knew the life I had lived as a child was like a guide to show me where I must work. It was not something to run away from.'

He paused for a moment and looked away, as though exhausted by the things he had said. The he turned back and continued: 'If you have no faith then maybe you cannot see it this way. But let me put it to you another way. I know that however much we suffered, there was happiness in my family. We were many and we all used to help each other and to fight and argue, all of that too, but above all we were together. There was always noise and laughter and warmth and people's voices in the house, not the silence I find in houses without children, like I have found in countries such as yours. Where is there happiness, Richards? In a community or a church or a family that is full of the voices of children, or in one where there is only the silence of their absence? And yet, as you tell me, we are already too many apparently for this poor, tired planet to support. There is the paradox, the reflection of our imperfection. But it does not make me give up hope. On the contrary, if I am to follow Christ, then I must live in hope, and it is only through his grace that there can by any hope....' He paused for a moment and then added 'This is a little too much like the priest making his sermon, isn't it?'

I did not say anything, but I felt that he was right and he knew it. For a moment it was as though he wanted to defuse the tension created by our discourse, but then he wound it tight again: 'It is also very serious and important to understand. The first temptation of Christ was to turn the stone into bread. That is maybe what your friends in the World Bank or all these other agencies may be thinking they can do and that is what it makes you angry, since you can see that what they want is impossible and they are arrogant to make these claims. But it is also wrong to be angry, at least to go on being angry. Perhaps a little anger can be good at first, just like a little good wine is good.'

He grinned, surprisingly, pausing to empty the last of the wine equally into both our glasses. Then he raised his glass, inviting me with a slight backward nod to do the same. We clinked them together and said the obligatory 'Salud!'

After the pause to swill the wine around his mouth and swallow it, he added in a voice that was altogether relaxed and conversational once more. 'Not everyone is bad or arrogant, thank God, and not everyone pretends they can make a perfect world. Now I think we have finished our meal.'

He stood up, signalling that I should remain where I was while he and Sister Lucy cleared the table. When this had been done and there was nothing left on the bare rough wooden surface, he disappeared into the back of the house.

Left alone, I watched the moths and smaller insect flutter round the paraffin lantern that hung from a nail slightly to one side of the table, casting a dim glow halfway across the room and leaving the rest in darkness. I thought about the things the priest had said. A lot of it was easy enough to see where it came from. The subtext would always have to be the line about the poor always being with you. As far as the Church was concerned, ending world poverty was not the game. It never had been. In a way the Church needed the poverty and the misery of it all to make its own place meaningful.

These thoughts came quickly into my mind and I chased them away impatiently. They were the tired and obvious thoughts that anyone could have and use and they did not provide any answers. I badly wanted to smoke. When I looked inside myself again I found that what had remained fixed and unmoving from the things that Father Severino had said was a single image, a picture of young children in a broken down hut made of corrugated iron, the sort I had seen everywhere I had been, and a baby born dead and then buried in a cardboard shoe box. I wondered if they had given the baby a name or if it had even been christened. I did not know what the rules of the Church would be in such cases or what they believed would happen to its immortal soul. Would it go to heaven unbaptised? The very strangeness of this question made me pause. I knew at once that it was not something I would ever ask the priest.

At that moment Father Severino returned, bring with him a half-full bottle of Scotch. He sat down and said 'We should finish our meal with something for our digestion.'

Sister Lucy came in from the kitchen with two shot glasses, the she set down on the table in front of us. For a moment she hovered, gazing hard at the two men doing something she did not like. Then she retreated, leaving us alone. Father Severino filled both glasses almost to the brim and then put the bottle down at arm's length from both of us. 'I am glad you have come, Richards,' he said. 'I knew from the moment I met you that you were someone special. And I know that you will do a lot to help the people in this places and maybe in other places like later, afterwards. I know it is in your heart. But there is a great bitterness inside you now that blocks out everything else. It comes out in everything you say and it makes you weak and full of doubt...' He paused and took a sip of the whisky, rolling it round his mouth before swallowing in an irritating, sacerdotal manner. Then he added 'Will you tell me about it?'

I had been expecting this moment, without thinking about it or preparing myself in any way, possibly from the moment I had met Father Severino and everything we had said to each other in the course of the evening had, I knew, been leading up to it. But that did not mean that I would willingly open doors I had closed a ling time ago. 'There's not a lot to tell,' I said, raising my glass to my lips.

The whisky tasted warm in my mouth. I swilled it around slowly before swallowing, imitating the priest only half-consciously and unsure as to whether there was any intention of mockery in what I did.

The priest said nothing in reply and the two of us sat in silence for a period of time neither of us was measuring, facing each other across the table and slowly drinking the whisky in our glasses. When the glasses were empty he unscrewed the bottle and filled them again almost to the rim. 'Salud, Richards,' he said, raising his glass.

'Salud, Father,' I said automatically, clinking my glass against the priest's and then taking a swig. Across the table in the semi-darkness of the lamplight the heavy mestizo features of the priest's face made it look quite different from what it had done in the sunlight earlier on. It was old and tired now, like a lumpy, ugly statue, as though the weight of what he had taken on, the years of lonely neglect and frustration in a forgotten corner of a large and troubled continent that awaited him, was already in possession of him and showing through from the inside.

My refusal to talk about myself seemed suddenly like an act of intense selfishness. It was as if I were refusing to reach out and help a man who was drowning in a lake too big to swim.

'Father,' I began.

'Listen Richards, my friend. You do not have to say more than you want to.' He reached across the table and touched my forearm in a gesture like a man calming a close friend he sees about to get emotional in a public place.

'It's alright, Father,' I interrupted in turn, speaking urgently now and finding an increasing fluency flowing into my mind and mouth with each word, like the fresh flow of a river long blocked. 'I do want to tell you. I'm just not sure where to begin.'

'Then start with what is important, the thing that is in your mind most often.'

'My mind is full of memories, Father. I seem to live with them more than I do in the present. At least, that is the way it seems at times.'

'Isn't that the same of all of us to some extent?'

'I don't know. How should I know, anyway? I have always seen it through my own eyes, not other people's. Things have happened and they tie me to the past. Other people seem to live more ordinary lives. They do things, they react to what goes on around them, they get on with whatever this business is that people have to do, they talk to each other and go to parties. But for me it is as though every breath I take comes from somewhere else. I see pictures of past things like a window in front of the real things going on here and now. And sometimes I end up talking to the images, like some lonely old head-case.'

I half expected the priest to pronounce some worn-out pious platitude at this point. I knew there was a tension inside me that was waiting to turn to anger. If the wrong words were spoken now they would stop the flow of words and it would not start again.

But the rough, dark features on the face across the table remain unmoving. Outside the insect chorus seemed to grow shriller and tenser in the darkness while we let the silence hang between us. For several minutes Father Severino sat looking at his glass without moving, as though, like me, he was lost in the world of images.

Then he looked up and said: 'We are both lonely men, Richards, and the world can be a very big place with nowhere that feels like home. I will never have a home in that ordinary sense. That is my calling and you could say I find my comfort in my daily routine of prayer and devotion, my iron coat of discipline, such as it is. But I don't talk to myself, I talk to God. Even then, it doesn't always work. Sometimes I don't feel anything. I do no hear a reply and I might as well be talking to myself, like the lonely old what-did-you-say? I too feel very lonely, very lost at times like those, alone and ever frightened. The world is a big, strange place and bad things happen.' He paused and took a breath and then continued 'But you do not have this calling of a priest. You do not have to live alone. Is there no-one in your life, no wife, no woman?'

'I was married, Father,' I said. I could hear my own voice, flat and clear, emphasising the past tense monosyllable, like a statement that someone else was reading out. 'A wife and child, in fact. But that was a long time ago. I lost them. They died. In an accident.'

The voice fell silent. In my mind it continued. It told about the images that came every night and often during the waking hours too, suddenly appearing, bright picture postcard memories of specific inconsequential moments lived long ago in that other time and place that could now perhaps be just a day's walk away across the border. It told about the way they looked at me with unblinking, searching eyes and how their lips moved with something they needed to tell me, some urgent message which I could not hear, because of the deafness, like a barrier that kept me from them.

But none of these words came out and I heard myself saying in a voice that did not really seem to come from my lips that I missed them.

Father Severino reached across the table once more and gripped my arm, this time not letting go at once but squeezing firmly. 'That is hard,' was all he said. Then he reached for the bottle once more and refilled our glasses in silence.

After we had drunk a bit more he spoke again, as if there had been no interruption and his words flowed directly on from what he had said before. 'I suppose it may be some time since they died. I will not ask you when, but I can imagine also that in that time people, perhaps many people have advised you to forget what is past and to move on and find someone else. But I don't think you want to hear those words from me, Richards. I can feel it in the way you speak and in the things you do not tell me, too.' He smiled the same gentle smile again. It was a smile that some people might have taken to be an expression of his inner personality, naively open like a shared book, exposing himself without concern for the risk or consequence.

'Don't worry,' he went on. 'It is not for me to give advice like that, like you find in some newspaper. For me, I will tell you that everyone has to carry his own cross. Even before I became this thing that I am now I remember my mother told me that. She had to carry hers till the day she died. Maybe she was wrong, though, maybe she was too proud and stubborn. Maybe she was right not to listen to people, but she also forgot to listen to God. God is always there, Richards, and one day with his help there can be a way.'

'And if I don't listen to him? What if I don't believe in him?'

'Most people don't and I do not know the answer. We change, we see things differently and he is always there. And you have friends, or one day, without expecting it, you may suddenly meet someone who is special for you. You know that and you believe it. It is what keeps you from giving up all hope. Has nothing like that happened to you since you lost your wife, even something you did not want or could not respond to?'

I could feel the whisky now, working its effect, warming my senses and at the same time dulling them, slowing my mind to the speed of a slow motion movie-sequence. 'I don't know Father,' I said and I could hear the weariness in my own voice, in the words that seemed to come from deep down below the levels where specific origin mattered. 'Memories have become very important to me. I sometimes feel they mean more than life itself, if by life you mean the things that go on day after day and the people that surround you just through coincidence or because they work with you or happen to be there where you are. I guess in a way, though, the happy memories are the things you cling to because they keep it from all falling apart when the going gets rough and the years go past and things start making less sense.

'I have memories, Father, sometimes very intense ones. I remember my childhood. I grew up in a small village in a bleak farming area, flat as a pancake and all mud in winter. It had no charm, no tourist attractions. But it was my home and I created a world out of it the way that children do. On Sundays when I was a little boy I used to sing in the church choir. My closest friends were in it too. We had a red-bearded choir master who made us sing the Mozart Ave Verum Corpus in a competition. Do you know that piece? It's very simple and also very beautiful, I would even say sublime. I still carry that tune in my head...' My eyes tracked away from the priest across the table, as though I had let my mind drift away to another place where the music rang our loud from the children's voices in an old, stone building. Then I looked down again and the sharp movement of my head seemed to shake me back to wakefulness. 'Anyway,' I said. 'We had a good time. After church I'd be waiting for Sunday lunch. I'd be shelling fresh peas and picking gooseberries and currants from the bushes at the end of our garden. There'd always be a roast leg of lamb or a joint of beef with gravy. My father would carve it and I'd count the peas on my plate and those on my brother's because I was always convinced he had more.

'Why I do remember this, Father? What is the point? It seems so inconsequential, but somehow, I find I cling onto these moments like I need them.'

Father Severino did not say anything in answer to my questions. Instead he unscrewed the top of the whisky bottle again and refilled our glasses. Having done this slowly and carefully with a steady hand, he raised his own glass to his lips, looking across the table, still silent.

We drank in silence for a few moments, the same way we had for each refill, as though it were a ritual. Then he said 'I don't know, Richards. I don't have answers to your questions. I am here to listen to whatever you want me to hear, but I do not have answers to everything. That would be a mistake. Sometimes listening is the most important thing… ' His voice drifted away and then, after a pause, he said 'I do know memories are important. Of course they are. They should be beautiful, maybe because they are what make us the thing we have become. But I know also that you have to live in the place you are and live the life of the person you have become, too. If you are going to be of any use to those around you who need you, you have to live with them and through them. And that means you cannot live inside a dream about the past.'

I had the impression that Father Severino's speech was just a little bit slurred, not so that you would have worried about it, but enough to make it apparent that he was sliding with me into the featureless terrain – wilfully following the path that led there – where something more profound might be revealed than could ever be achieved among the wholly sober.

'It's easy for you to say that, Father,' I said. 'Everybody likes you. How could anybody not like a person like you? I can see the people around here adore you. They need you, you see. You bring them the hope they never had or had lost through all these years of war off and on, displacement, wandering and staying at the bottom of the heap. I can see how they need you, Father. I saw it from the first. It's in the way they look at you and sing and dance when you show up.

'But they don't need me, Father. I am just a minor bureaucrat, more washed-out than I usually care to admit, making a living out of all that they have to suffer…

'And besides,' I added, feeling the anger rising inside, raising my heartbeat and loosening my tongue. 'I do have my nightmares, the ones that keep me awake at night and give me no rest. Or is that being too dramatic? It may just be the whisky talking through me!

'I see them, you see, standing where I left them at the airport. They are trying to say something to me. I don't know what it is, but I know it is important. But I cannot hear them. It's as though they were behind a great thick sheet of plate glass.

'You know, Father, at times I think memories are like stars in a vast, empty universe. Did I say that already, I don't remember? Anyway, they all have a different mass and so a different gravitational attraction. Some are so massive they can capture you permanently or pretty nearly. You are like a small body, trapped in orbit. That is how it is.'

I paused to drink some more. I was reckless now with the whisky and it did not seem to matter what I said, what should be shared and what would be better kept to myself alone. The images came into my mind hot and alive and I felt it to be nothing more than a gateway through which they could pass in order to be born in the words that flowed with a coherence that was entirely mystical out through my mouth. 'I remember the first time I swam in the Indian Ocean. The sea was warm, like a bath it seemed to me. I was so young, Father, and so lonely, stuck out in some village in Central Province teaching in a Harambee school. At Easter time I hitchhiked my way down to Mombasa. Got a ride with a kombi full of Sikhs who took me to the temple at Makindu – you know you can still get a free lunch there? Vegetarian, but really good stuff. To me back then, first time out in the big wide world away from England, it was like stepping inside the Arabian Nights or the album sleeve of Sergeant Pepper, surrounded by guys in turbans all eating curry with chapattis. Anyway, I ended up camping on this beach down south of the Likoni ferry with a bunch of people older than myself. The ocean was warm, like blood, like I told you, so warm it excited you, made you feel free and far away from whatever your life and childhood had been back in the cold, dark places. I remember we sat there up to our necks in the warm sea smoking enormous spliffs. One of the guys had a rubber tube so he could blow it rights down into your lungs… Afterwards, some days later, when I had to leave to go back to my work at the school, I found I could not control my emotions, they were somehow much stronger than before and for no reason I was in tears, floods of tears, taking the bus up into town across the ferry to find the Nairobi road and start hitching back to my village.

'Why do I remember this now? And why am I telling you, Father? It is not important, just self-indulgent junk. But it's funny, the way every memory is linked up. Every time I have let things go too far, let my emotions escape so that I spout whatever crap is inside me or laugh too much or cry or get too friendly or loud, whatever it is, every time I do that, I end up hating myself. I'll wake up in the morning wishing I was dead – no, I really mean it, not just words, but inside the disgust is so strong I don't now want to think or feel this conscious mind anymore. And the memory of every time I have been like that is always there with me, reminding me of how useless I am and how pointless my life is.'

I stopped and carefully pushed the glass away along the table. Then I said very carefully: 'And I don't want that to happen now. I want to stop here.'

'We will have one more glass.' The voice that came from Father Severino's lips was not gentle. It had harsh quality that was more brown-skinned Mexican indio than mestizo, something that came from the ones who got pissed so bad they could not walk, straight from the trash pile alley-ways where a still-born child might get buried in a shoe-box. It challenged me and threw the preconceived notions and first impressions right back at me.

Father Severino slowly filled the two glasses. 'This is number four,' he said. 'Or maybe number five. We are not drunk and this is not the night to pretend to be a little old lady. You are not here to tell lies to yourself or to anybody else. You are in the confessional, remember.' With these words his smile returned, gentle as before. 'Now let the whisky lubricate your memory a little, my friend,' he said. 'And then you can tell me something good, the hope you have. There must be someone in your life. You are not old, Richards. Someone must have come into your life, even if your eyes were closed at the time.'

'Will it help if I talk about things that don't even exist, except perhaps in my mind? Come on, Father, don't ask me to make things up. Of course there have been some relationships, none of them worth the time it took to get in a tangle and then untangle it again. Some women are looking for trouble, it seems, or maybe a challenge and I suppose that is what I am. And I won't say I didn't try at time or didn't care for anyone. I am not like that, I mean. I do care and I have tried. But the feeling never comes – you know, love. I can't feel that. It just is not there, there's no capacity, it seems, and I always end up disappointing or hurting whoever it is who's decide that I am the man for them. It always ends badly and in the end I prefer just not to try. I can't just pretend.'

Inside I could feel a deep unhappiness opening up the way it always did, like the endless plain on whose expanse I knew my soul was already lost.

'Look Father,' I said, 'this does not signify anything at all. It's just the whisky talking and making stupid conjectures out of small and insignificant things. There simply isn't anyone in my life and there doesn't have to be a reason. It's just the way things turned out after I lost the ones I did have.' I felt irritated now. The half-formed idea I had of making some sort of act of confession, which would clear out all the nightmare stuff that cluttered up my mind, was turning into something stupid, verging on the prurient, like some vulgar tabloid interrogation, bound to end up with a load of cheap, sanctimonious advice that would not help at all.

'Maybe life is not that way with you these days, Richards.' The priest was still smiling, but the smile looked imbecilic now, deeply irritating in its failure to realize the extent of my humiliation. 'At least you must have friends you can rely on?'

For the first time there was something verging on doubt in his tone of voice, as though he had joined me on the edge of territory that was wholly unfamiliar. Because of course the third-world people, the people like his own vast family and these villagers he worked with here, all lived surrounded by one another, by the noise, the voices, the arguments, the smells of one another. And the idea of a life lived wholly alone, in the absence not only of other people, but also God, must be to them a near approximation to hell. I smiled at this thought. This time my reply would not just be a negation of his own existence, it would be a strength and a weapon, my weapon. It would hurt outwards as well as inwards.

'No, Father,' I said quietly, letting my smile show. 'I have no-one.'

"That is a terrible condition, Richards.' I thought I could detect an emotional tremor in Father Severino's voice as he said this and I was aware that it pleased me.

'No, Father,' I said. 'I do not ask for anything more. What should I look for in any case? Besides,' I reached across and clutched his sleeve the way he had done to me before, 'you must be pretty much alone too.'

'I have God!' Father Severino spoke with a sudden vehemence that almost knocked me off my balance. 'I told you I have my calling!'

I looked at him for a while recovering my poise before I spoke, quite calmly and quietly. 'And I have nothing.' That is what these words and this silence imply. 'I see the sunrise and taste the rain. One day it will be switched off and that will be the end.'

'The end?'

'Rest, maybe. Quiet. Nothing more.'

For a few moments we lapsed into silence again, but it was a silence charged with awkward energy, an absence of harmony that cried out to be brought to an end. Then Father Severino emptied his glass with a final swig and said firmly 'We end here tonight.'

He stood up, extending a hand towards me. 'We say goodnight now, although I know our business is not finished, Richards. I hope tomorrow will bring you inspiration when we visit the village of the Jiye. You will see the work there is for your to do, the many good things there are when people have so little…Hope is never lost.'

'Yes, Father, thank you.'

I said this submissively, aware that I was still, if only just, on the sober side of the line and wanting hard not to spoil the good things there were between us. Then I stood up, shook hands with the priest and stepped out into the black, insect-ridden night.

## 5.

*Sunday Morning*
Without a torch I blundered uncertainly, in part because of the whisky I had been drinking, but more because of the utter blackness of the night through which I was trying to find my way. There was no lighting of course, not even the glow of a cheap Chinese paraffin lamp or the dying embers of a fire. I knew the way and it was simple, straight on down the track that came from the plateau up above and petered out on the edge of the landing strip, from the far side of which the rough road that connected this place to the highway south to the border picked up again. The SRRC compound was no more that a couple of hundred yards in a straight line along this track, but every blind, shuffling, uncertain step seemed to add another minute onto the time it took to arrive at the wooden frame of the gateway, beyond which I could hear the voices of my colleagues, still seated round the fire over by the kitchen hut beyond the row of tents.

From the gate I could clearly see their faces lit up by the glow of the fire. I was aware of being glad to see them with a feeling that was almost contrition. In this version of events my visit to the house of the priest to sit and eat at a table spread with a clean cloth had been a betrayal of our mission, a way of copping out from shared hardship that now must diminish my standing with my colleagues. I also knew that a big part of the feeling that contributed to the sense of guilt and the desire it gave me to make amends and somehow worm my way back into the group I despised was a sense of disgust for the experience of the evening. I had created a flimsy artifice out of the things I desired to clarify inside and had given myself the impression that I had found a guide or mentor in the priest, when what I had really been seeing was just the projection of my own need for that person in the face of a reality that had been something different.

I was not sure how I would define the priest now. There was a strength in him alright and a sureness of purpose from which it stemmed and on which it fed, but that in itself was not enough. There was something verging on crassness in his lack of sensitivity. He was a mechanic in a priest's vestments, nothing more, and the strength he had was rooted in a simplicity that could not provide any protection against the demons, because it did not understand them and probably did not even see them.

The men sitting round the fire stopped talking as I emerged out of the darkness to join them. I looked round the circle of their faces, half expecting to see a row of openly hostile scowls glaring back at me from the low camp stools and half-broken wooden office chairs they were seated on, but instead finding only the wide smiles of welcome on the faces of John and Samuel that I had long taken for granted. Simon was wearing his customary smile that said nothing. Only Daniel looked away, refusing to make eye contact, and that was hardly surprising.

'Sit down with us, Richards,' said John. 'We were just talking about politics, as usual.' He laughed. His voice was deep and rich, the voice of a large man, and his laughter sounded self-assured and self-deprecating at the same time. This was their land and their way of doing things, the talk would never end, unchanging, endless as the to and fro movement of the herds across the toic, westward towards the high ground in the rains, east towards the river in the dry.

'Any developments?' I asked, by way of making conversation as I sat down on a tree log that was the only remaining seat.

'Francis Deng may be coming to South Sudan.'

'The big man, eh?'

I knew it was not clever, but I could not keep the sarcasm out of my voice. Another self-important elder statesman was coming to the pow-wow to claim his share of adulation from an admiring crowd vibrant with expectations that they desperately needed to hang around some other person's - some leader's - neck, so that he could pull them forwards like oxen to the promised land where they would find the sense of unified purpose the needed to make their own way.

'Everyone wants him to come. He is respected by everyone. If he comes it will be a good sign for the peace process.'

'Always looking for signs…'

John and Samuel laughed. There was no malice in their laughter. They saw things I could not. They did not really expect me to follow the meanderings of the herd the way their people had always done. To the Dinka and the Nuer drovers it was as obvious and inevitable as the course of the sun across the vast sky or the coming of the rains.

I knew this as well as they did. I could easily remember the hours spent during my first few months, sometimes during the long flights across the empty landscapes, reading whatever I could to try to understand the mess I was here to work on and with, the twenty or thirty years of conflict, or was it two or three centuries? Deng's book was a great big fat one. He had once been a minister in a Sudanese government that included some intellectuals and leaders from the south. Now he was a respected academic in the United States, old enough to have acquired a higher status than almost anyone else across the grasslands, not that that made it any less hard to see what a visit by him would achieve. In all honesty I could not really see what any of the many gestures and missions were meant to achieve. They all added up to something, but I had long given up trying to follow the way the politics of peace worked.

Simon was smoking. He proffered the packet of Ethiopian Nyalas, so I took one, gratefully, lighting it with a burning twig plucked from the edge of the fire.

'So,' he said, 'you did not come for dinner. You stayed with the priest.' The interrogation in his tone was enough to make it clear that he wanted to hear whatever there was to tell about the evening spent at the mission house.

'Father Severino is a good man,' I said, cautiously, not wanting to commit myself too quickly to revealing the plans for the following day. It had not been established whether the SRRC's permission would be required for the trip or what powers Simon might have to forbid it if, for whatever reason, it did not please him or his masters.

'Yes,' said Simon emphatically, smiling round at everyone. 'He is a really great man. He is doing many things, many fine things here for the community.'

The others nodded in assent and it occurred to me that the only way to deal with the thing was to have things clear while there was harmony and we were pulling together.

'He was telling me about this Jiye village, the people displaced by Toposa cattle raiders. He wants us to go and take a look at them. I think it would be a good idea. We could include them in the assessment. In fact we ought to anyway.'

'Why not?' said Simon. 'I thought that was the plan already?'

'Yes, that's right.' I was taken aback to find Simon already so amenable. 'But he was just telling me a bit more - about their conditions and so on. I think we should all go – take a proper look at nutrition and sanitation and so on. There'll be room in the truck.'

'Of course,' said Simon again. 'I have to come. I am responsible for your safety.'

'Is it dangerous?' I felt a tightening in my stomach. The feeling was not apprehension or fear, more like the excitement of a child anticipating a visit to an adventure park with rides that might just do something more than merely take your breath away. Underneath it all, I wanted that thrill and I knew I had been searching for it all along. At some inner level right down at the bottom, deep down under the rationalised and intellectually justified layers, there existed a yearning for danger and risk that had drawn me to this theatre and this job. Everyone who worked in the programme in the field, whether for the UN or the NGOs, was tainted with it to some degree. It was what kept some NGO staff at Loki for years, like aged, deranged hippies hanging on at a rock festival campsite long after the event has come and gone, addicted to the music and the substances and unable to return to any other sort of life. It was not necessarily a bad thing, either. In fact it could be just what was needed to keep good professionals slogging away when the results were so meagre and the temptation to give up all hope of achieving anything so high. But for myself, I knew it had become something different. Solitary and unaccompanied by anything more positive to mollify its deadening influence, it had started to rot. I could feel this rottenness all the time, eating away at my spirit, destroying my ability to see beyond the darkness of the night to the light of the coming dawn. I wanted the danger, if it really did exist, for its own sake, whatever the consequences. It was no longer a spice but an end in itself and there was nothing to be sought beyond it.

'It may be. That cannot be told,' said Simon. His voice had changed suddenly, as though he had changed the mask he wore. It was solemn and it made me think he must relish the power that knowledge of bad and dangerous things conferred on him. 'The Jiye are not so very far, but it is down towards the south and if there are cattle raids, then it is dangerous.'

'The Toposa are dangerous,' said Samuel, 'like the Turkana around Loki.'

'Yes, but it's mainly cattle-raiding, isn't? They don't have any pro-government militias.' I said this firmly. I did not want to let the conversation go a single step down a path that might lead my colleagues to spook themselves now.

'But they are all armed. They all have AK47s.'

'Yes, but…'

'Don't worry, we are coming with you, Richards,' John interrupted, laughing as he had done before. 'We are not afraid. After so many years in the field! We've all been through many things. You know that Samuel used to be in the SPLM and I have been in the field for many years now, including during the time when the fighting was bad. I was once in a village when it was bombed by an Antonov…'

'How was that?'

'It was frightening. I was frightened like everybody else.' John paused to let the memory come to fill his mind. Then he went on, 'The sound of the planes comes first and then all the people running to the shelters, the children and the women screaming, screaming so loud they are almost as loud as the engines of the plane coming nearer, not very high – that is what is so bad, they do not fly very high. You are almost sure they are looking just for you and you want to cover yourself up and hide, like an ant on the ground.

'I ran too, of course. I did as we had been told to do. I jumped down into the shelter – we were in the SCF camp in Malwal Kon – every camp has to have a shelter. I jumped down into the trench and squatted down. I was scared as the plane went over. But we were safe.'

'When the militias raid, they have "technicals",' said Simon, 'with machine guns mounted at the back. They fire at everyone they see. They machine gun every house.'

'And grenade launchers…' said Samuel. 'I have seen it when I was in the SPLM. The government gives them so many weapons, so many…'

'They say the Chinese are arming them now. They want to kill everyone so they can take the oil without any resistance.'

'Fucking Chinese!' I had never met any of them but I knew I hated them, not the real flesh and blood people, perhaps, but the rapacity they came with that was gobbling up the people of the swamps like a story-book monster. I hated them the same way I hated the economists who said that this was the only way, the endless mantra of growth chanted in a listless chorus by the uncounted, faceless millions in a world grown so rich and at the same time grown so poor. There was no other story: one day you were out in the bush somewhere in the vast landscape tending your cattle, the next you were condemned to the sordid misery of a tin shack in a stinking shanty while somebody somewhere was using you as a statistic to say that you and people like you were better off. Or else you were homeless or maybe dead, because it was easier to get rid of you than to use you.

They all sat in silence for a few moments. Then John spoke again to ask if I had eaten already.

'Yes, they invited me to eat.'

'Sister Lucy cooks well,' said Simon. He was back in character now, distorting his smooth face with a salacious leer.

'Yes, it was very nice,' I said, suddenly feeling the effect of the whisky as the cigarette fumes got to my head, weighing it down with a heavy, throbbing ache. I knew at once what Simon was trying to suggest, but had no energy and no interest in responding. I just wanted to be alone and to sleep. 'I think I'll go to bed. It'll be a long day tomorrow.'

No-one else stirred as I got up and made my way over to my tent. I cleaned my teeth in the darkness and then zipped myself inside the canvass cocoon. I could hear their voices behind me, rising and falling in turn and occasionally in unison grunting agreement on some point as they returned to the conversation he had interrupted, the timeless, unending song of the toic made real and sharp by the politics of the moment, which were themselves no more than a repetition of a cycle that had last been played through half a century earlier.

…..

For now I was hoping that the fatigue of the day would combine with the effects of the alcohol to send me straight into a deep and dreamless sleep. I lay on his back on the camp bed in the hot night air. My head was spinning, just a little, with the dizziness brought on by the cigarette and the heaviness of the wine. It was not a bad feeling. Anything more and I would be hating it, feeling the reins of control slipping away from my hands and knowing that only time and rest could bring them back into my grasp. But this was fine, just a slight disequilibrium that told me to lie down and stare up at the sharp canvas slope above my head until sleep came. In the morning I would follow my own routine, rising early to wash, and then I would pack my rucksack with the kit I had laid out neatly along the other side of the tent. Its presence now was a comfort, part of a routine that took away the need to think beyond the mechanical activity required for comfort and survival. I reckoned I would have time to walk round to the church compound before the others rose to sit and wait for their breakfast.

I wanted to thank Father Severino and Sister Lucy for the meal and to check on the time of departure. There was more to it than that. The messy ending of our conversation troubled me, not so much because of the botched ending to my "confession" - I had not wanted to expose myself in that way, in any case. It had just been an impulse based on an instinctive sense of affinity for the man, not his official capacity or anything like that -, but because I could not work out or remember how things had ended on that instinctive level. Had it been good or bad? Would the morning bring only the awkwardness of two strangers who meet, get drunk, bare their souls and then wish they had never done so and hope they never have to face one another again?

I was sure Father Severino and Sister Lucy would not want to leave too late and if necessary I would be prepared to come back and wake the others up. For once I would not feel awkward about organizing them, bullying them and ordering them around. They themselves would understand the need to stick to the schedule and how if the drive was a lone one it could not be left till later. In that African way I had seen before, they would appear to be completely disorganized one moment and then catch me completely off guard the next by being ready to go and heading for the gate, while I would still have my pack open to re-check some piece of equipment I probably did not need and would end up running to catch up as they strolled out of the compound. I had found it a mystery at first, but now suspected it came from the simplicity of what they took with them, which looked pretty good and cool at first, but in fact meant that when the time came, when thirst began to bite or a long morning spent rambling around the ramshackle village brought on the fatigue and listlessness of hunger, they would be without food and without water and turning to me with an expectation that I would have these things that had no basis in right or formal allocation to tasks and responsibilities. It was just the way things seemed to be.

My thoughts wandered on, preventing the blanket of sleep I sought from covering my eyes and closing down my mind, out across the endless, flat, treeless expanses of Eastern Upper Nile, under a mountainous sky of grey clouds, from where the water poured in a merciless, unbroken torrent, to miserable, forsaken, back-of-beyond Kochkuon, where even the landing strip was under water. It had been in a Twin Otter that time. Any other plane would either have crashed on landing or failed to take off.

The journey did not stop. The weather changed, the people and the places were also different. My mind threw them together into one unbroken time and another place, an endless series of other places that were always the same in the end. I was flying to Ruweng County, low over the oilfields, laid out in chessboard squares, crossed by arrow-straight roads and dotted with neat installations, bereft of any sign of human life or human habitation.

The plane landed at Chokanat. The pilot was nervous. He told the team we had only an hour and a half on the ground. If we were not back within that time he would leave without us.

On the ground SPLA military were everywhere. A straggle of new poorly constructed huts stretched along the river bank. Cows were sitting down or lying on their sides all around, dying as we watched them. The people slowly gathered, ragged, suspicious, silent. There was no real community in this place, their being here was accidental. They had been displaced from their homeland by the oil fields. They had nothing, no school, no clinic, almost no food, just the cattle dying around them. They said their cattle were being killed by anthrax and foot and mouth imported by Falatta nomads, wandering as they always had done across the Sahel from their homeland in Nigeria.

The landscape was dry, a landscape of dust swirling around dried-out trees. The team had to walk fast to complete the assessment, trying to talk with the people we met, and the usual questions were in his mind about whether the obligatory presence of the local SRRC secretary, escorting us wherever we went, was a help or a hindrance. You could not really reach the ragged people, anyway, on one of these quick missions. They were just faces that you might forget, but which you would try to firm into an impression that would stay, partly made up of the official stuff you noted down about water and food and disease and crops and partly the image you would try to fix inside your mind. Sometimes you took photographs and if they came out well, you would share them in the office or put them in the report, but they would fade from sight in the end. The mental picture mattered more.

The plane took off again without pilot or flight plan through the empty air and up over the featureless landscape of the past, chasing the pinpricks of memory like the white of the landing strips laid out in the sandy soil below. My heart filled with a deep melancholy as I flew across the big, empty, unchanging world. The rain was like a curtain now, pulled down to close the swamplands off from the outside world. In some little stations, long-serving aid workers, homesick and desperate to see their families or burning up with malaria, would watch as the plane sent to pick them up circled the landing strip once or maybe twice under the heavy grey rain clouds, only to turn and head off into the sky. It took a strong and resolute personality to stay out there year on year. A lot of them only managed it through developing a deep religious faith that tied them into one of the myriad of charismatic and evangelical churches that Africa seemed to love and to create so easily.

Down again at a small airstrip, no different from the rest, Mayendit, a tiny dot in the middle of the grasslands and reed beds. Dr. Melchior was there, unexpectedly, presiding over a meeting inside a dark, unlit hut.

As I entered from the bright sunlight the darkness of the interior blinded me. The sinister, smooth voice of Dr. Melchior invited me to sit down next to him and I shuffled clumsily towards the low table at the far end of the room. My eyesight slowly returned to reveal that the place was jam-packed, mainly with men, sitting on the floor or on low, wooden benches. The atmosphere was thick and fetid. There was no-one outside, where the landscape was pancake flat and empty all the way to the village some two miles away. Everybody was here inside, in the dark with Dr. Melchior.

I sat down on the chair next to Dr. Melchior, not noticing the dog at his feet, a long-haired, very white creature of indeterminate breed. It looked up at me, snarled and then started to growl continuously in a low monotone. Dr. Melchior smiled, displaying the curious gap between his front teeth common to so many Nuer and Dinka men. I knew it was the result of the ritualistic removal of six teeth. I found myself slipping nervously into an academic consideration of this point, when Dr. Melchior's voice brought me back to where I was, telling me in soft, almost soothing tones that the dog did not like white people. There was no way to judge whether he said this in earnest or not. His dark glasses made it hard to see expression in the greater darkness of the hut. But the dog growled and strained at the short leash that secured it to the leg of its master's chair, while its master continued to smile slowly and to stare through his dark glasses at his guest.

Who was Dr. Melchior? Maybe he was the turncoat leader of a tribal faction made famous by a massacre more than ten years before, carving in his lust for power a division between the peoples of the south that still had not been healed? Or was he in fact one of the players in the endgame that everyone thought was now in sight? How did you tell? A recanting sinner, returning to the fold after years of playing games with the enemy? Or neither of these things, just a played-out-has-been out to make a bit more trouble in a bid to stake a claim to a share of the spoils?

Maybe you could be all these things.

For now he was just asking, politely and quietly with a gapped-tooth smile and his eyes hidden behind dark glasses in the heavy fug of a windowless hut – asking for a food drop to be made to support his next reconciliation meeting and then, with no apparent awareness of the bathos in this demand for something so small and simple following so hard on the request for the big-time manna from the sky, for a pad of paper. It seemed the judge working with him had already used up what little they had had at the outset.

That was part of the tragedy of South Sudan, it seemed. Out in its vastness, not even a leader who thought he mattered had access to such a simple item as paper to write on.

Night came upon us rapidly once the day's flying was over. The air was full of insects. In my hut at the camp at Nyal the torchbeam revealed large spiders sitting silently on the walls. At dinner one of the local Unicef staff put on the video of Congolese pop music that she had brought with her – gyrating women, fat men wearing shades, swimming pools and Mercedes cars, a strange parade of all the things most Africans did not have and never would have.

At one point I sat up, abruptly shaken into full wakefulness by a memory sharper than the rest. Dr. Melchior was in the darkness, sitting in his tent in Lavington, talking smoothly about the politics of peace with a fat little man from UN headquarters. The visitor was nervous. He wanted to leave, to get back to his safe hotel room in Westlands, but the rain was falling hard outside in the garden and he did not have an umbrella. Dr. Melchior knew this. He could see it all and he was laughing with his eyes.

And later, much later, just a month or two before this trip, I had been on my way to the Princess Zarah Pavilion at the Aga Khan Hospital. I remembered how it occurred to me to wonder who Princess Zarah was. Her 'pavilion' was a smart new building with comfortable, air-conditioned private room. I was going to see a woman I had met some time before in Rumbek, an anthropologist. Someone had told me she was ill. I did not know her well, but I was going to see her.

I found her looking haggard. She was on a drip. She had been badly dehydrated. But more than her physical condition it was her mental stated that had got to me. Her mind was full of darkness, as though the long weeks alone in the toic had entered it and taken possession.

I knew she had been at Dr. Melchior's camp in Upper Nile. She had been sponsored in some way by the American embassy. Something had gone wrong, something more than simply falling ill from the water or the bite of an insect. Her sponsors had sent the plane to fetch her a week before it was due and the flight had been classified as a medevac. I had heard about it all in the course of his work during one of my routine meetings with the donor representatives and had accepted the suggestion that I visit her on behalf of the team. The man from the embassy who had told me I should go and see her had said she had a history of erratic behaviour and had showed signs of being subject to delusions on previous occasions.

I sat down by her bed and asked how she was doing. She started talking almost at once, as though I had come to take a statement from her. Maybe that was what she believed. I had not explained my reason for being there and would not have known what to say if she had asked. I did not really know if I was simply driven by curiosity or some compassionate, pastoral instinct that went with the responsibilities of my job. It had simply seemed natural that I should want to see her.

She said she had believed she knew Dr. Melchior well enough and could speak her mind with him. In some discussion she had told him bluntly that he and his cronies should face the fact that the Government had won the war since it now had all the oil it wanted and could get all the weapons it wanted. Maybe he had changed sides again at just the wrong moment. Somehow this unguarded remark, spoken in the course of some argument no more exceptional in her mind than any of the other inconclusive discussions about the war and the peace in which she had taken part or which she had sat and watched, had offended him more that she had expected. It had seemed to touch some new and very raw sensitivity. Maybe she had got it right about this falling out, or maybe it was just the product of an overwrought imagination, driven in on itself alone in the middle of the swamps with no company other than an angry warlord and his henchmen, but she had been shaken and she was still very frightened, even here safely back in Nairobi, in the "Pavilion".

Out in the cattle camp she had become convinced Melchior was trying to poison her. He had had bath water delivered to her tent that stung her skin where she used it and then gave her five hand-rolled cigarettes. She understood enough of the Nuer language to listen to the whispering voices in the darkness outside her tent at night and to distinguish fragments of a hurried conversation that frightened her. Someone had said 'Don't smoke the cigarettes given to the woman!' and had then gone on to giver orders for her to be given separate water to drink at the next meal – water with something special in it.

Later they brought her a cup of coffee which she was sure had been poisoned. She waited until they had gone and then poured it onto the ground inside her tent where no-one could see her.

So it had continued for days. She was no longer sure how many, the better part of a week, maybe more, maybe two weeks. In the end when the small plane came for her, she felt she had only just escaped. She was sure the cigarettes and water had been infused with pyrethrum. She had only smoked half of one of the cigarettes and had brought the remainder back with her so that they could be subjected to toxicological tests. She told me the hospital had promised to do them so that she could prove her case to the embassy. They would have to do something then, take some action, make a denunciation.

In her hospital bed she looked haunted more than sick, as if she feared something or someone bad might enter the room at any moment. I had tried to imagine her alone in the swamps for days on end, half-understanding the sinister whispering voices in the dark outside, wondering about the stories told about the use of insecticides to eliminate enemies and wondering if this was to be her fate. I thought of the smile that danced on the face of Dr. Melchior behind his dark glasses. Sudan could so easily become a collection of horror stories, some buried, others uncovered, a history of great misery and great evil. There was so much darkness in the swamps.

I lay in the darkness, thinking again now of the woman, frail and twisted in the bed, her lips cracked and her face contorted with a pain that was not physical. What was it I had felt as I sat by her bedside? I could not tell. Perhaps the stirring of something I thought I had left behind, beyond simple compassion, something else that had lingered in the unexamined area of my mind since the time I had met her under the warm night sky at the Afex camp by the Rumbek landing strip. After the first meeting I had thought about her as I read the Evans Pritchards books I had bought. I had never done the things the anthropologists did. I had not gone to live for months on end alone in the swamps. I had always thought I would like to do that, but life had never given me the space or the opportunity. That was what I told myself when I looked back, knowing that it would not convince my listening other self which knew too well the history of failure and defeat, of a flawed inner being behind the course that I had made good. Now I had come to see the challenge of solitude in a different way. It was an end in itself. The swamps were simply there before me every time, challenging and luring me into a darker contest with myself and with the dark angels and demons that waited for me in the darkness.

And yet there had been something more about the image of the woman in my mind, a confusion beyond the male protective instinct, perhaps even, if I was honest enough to admit it, something more that a man might want from what he might have and share with a woman. The thought had been exciting. It was not hard to tell myself that I did not enjoy the loneliness into which my intellect was driving me. The visceral self still longed to escape back into the warmth of a live lived with and for and in other people. I was sure I had known that state before, however imperfectly, and I was aware, when being honest with myself, that behind this lack of hesitation in accepting the suggestion that I should visit the woman in hospital, it was this other thing that in part was driving me.

I had dismissed it all easily enough with a shrug when she told me she was heading home to the States as soon as she was well…

I rolled over a few times, twisting my kikoy into a series of uncomfortable knots around my loins. It would not do, I told myself. I could not let this drift of images continue, denying me the sleep I had promised myself. I sat up and swung my legs sideways together onto the ground. Then I twisted in one movement round into a kneeling position and fumbled my way to the entrance of the tent.

Outside it was quiet now. The others were in their tents and Simon had gone home. The final embers of the fire still glowed where a thicker log had burnt only halfway through. The sky above was dark the way it only can be when there are no electric lights for many miles around. The stars glittered bright as jewels and close. I stepped out and zipped the tent flap behind me. Then I switched on the small electric torch I carried in my hand and made my way carefully across the open yard to the corrugated iron shack that housed the long-drop toilet. I did not like to go there in the dark. The spiders that sat motionless on the wall seemed to be waiting for me, as though I were a fly. But I did not want to relieve myself behind the trees over by the gate, as I could so easily have done. It was a question of principal, right or wrong, that had become axiomatic, the need to practice what we all preached, the elementary lessons of hygiene and public health. Because if it did not have sufficient value to mean you would stick to it yourself then what was the value of it at all? And once you started to question the underlying values, then the whole edifice came tumbling down on top of you and the sense of purpose that still flickered, like a dying flame inside your soul, could well go out.

I compromised the way I usually did in the dark, keeping the door open and standing on the threshold to urinate into the hole in the ground. That way I could keep an eye on the spiders and back out quickly if they started to move.

I washed my hands with water from the bucket that stood half-full next to the plastic jerry-can. Then I looked up at the stars. My head felt clear now and the air was cooler than it had been earlier, as the intense heat of the day dissipated under the open sky. It would be good to stay outside for a while, to let the images inside the tent dissipate, too, before going back inside. Right now they would be waiting for me in there, like the spiders.

I felt small and afraid, the way the dark always made you feel. I looked to the familiar patterns of the stars to bring the comfort they always had done. When I was still a child I had learnt their names and the names of the shapes that the imaginations of men had grouped then into. In those days I had been gazing out of a bedroom window into the gap between the prickly mess of branches of an aging cherry plum tree and the apple tree that stood further away, the last remnant of what had once been an orchard. I had always been scared of the dark. When I was very small I would cry out and my father or my mother would come, but they had become increasingly unwillingly to do so as I grew older and so I had had to look for other friends to comfort me, finding the stars in a book and then in the sky outside, bright and infinitely strong, far away, yet close enough to be with me every night. Now there was nothing left apart from them, brighter here than anywhere else, but still constant, still the same.

There had been a long time during which I had asked for death, wandering around a cold garden in the dark, praying out loud, if that was what it could be called, talking to a God who never answered and who I had never really thought of beyond the rituals of childhood and school. But that was long ago in the immediate aftermath of what had happened, when all I could think of was the hole left in my life that I had never thought I would have to try to fill again. Now there was nothing, just the monotony of being alone and the unconvincing comfort I had taught myself to find in the certainty of my mortality.

I started to head back towards the line of tents. Daniel was twiddling the knobs on his radio again with the volume turned down low. I could hear the earnest whine of some American preacher, but I could not make out the words. He was probably missing his family, the wife and small children who were waiting for him in far-away Nairobi. It was easier when you did not have any, much easier – for someone like me. Of course, it had been different once, but it was hard now to capture the sense of it all, the feeling of coming home to a place shared with someone else, someone you loved and took for granted as part of everything you were and did.

In the early days when we were very much in love, I would walk in at the door and smile, because I knew she liked my smile, and she would stroke the hair back from my forehead and kiss me. Then we would sit down at the small kitchen table and talk about what we had done during our separate days. She had names for me that no-one else did and I would not have wanted to hear them from anyone else. But from her it sounded good, like the touch of her fingers on the skin of my face.

In Ethiopia the people had had a funny way of pronouncing my name, so that Richards came out as 'Wretched'. I had found it funny until after the accident. Then it had come to seem only too appropriate, like a bad dream or a prophecy come true.

Leaving my plastic flip-flops under the fly-sheet, I unzipped the mosquito-netted inner tent flap and got inside quickly in order to close it again before any insects could follow. I straightened the kikoy around my legs, lay down on the camp bed and switched the torch off. I felt tired now, back out of the time tunnel and into the dark velvet void where sleep beckoned and said 'Be still and rest.' I lay for a few moments breathing slowly, calmly, thinking of nothing until my eyes closed of their own accord and I was gone.

Some time before dawn they came to me, the way they always did. They were standing in a large public building, the departures hall of an airport. That was where they always came to find me. They were leaving and I was not sure if it was a good thing or a bad thing. She was wearing the long white woollen coat she always wore when the weather was cold and the beret she had bought when we first arrived in London, deep crimson on top of the deep, lush darkness of her hair. The child was wearing denim dungarees with a little red jacket over the top. I could remember going to buy those clothes together and stopping in Sloane Square to have tea in the café she used to like going to at the top of Peter Jones, from where you could look out in the early winter darkness at the lights down below. She was holding the child's hand and they were both looking at me, hard and serious. They were saying something, the words they always said which I could never hear. I knew I had to listen hard and then maybe I might catch the sound of their voices, but something got in the way and kept me from going nearer to her. I could feel it, like strong arms pulling me back. They began to fade, turning slightly as if about to walk away. I lunged forward desperately and found myself awake, sweating and hot with fever.

I reached for the torch and checked my watch. 5 a.m. Still almost two hours of darkness to go. I swigged water from the plastic bottle I had left beside my head and then lay back.

It was always like this. If an image from a dream was strong in my mind at the moment of waking it would stay and with it every detail of the dream – long enough at least for me to write it down if I had ever wanted to. I could see them both quite clearly now in my mind's eye. It was not hard to remember the life we had had together, especially the final years in Ethiopia, in the country that started just across the border from where I now lay.

I had been working hard then, taking it all too seriously, waging a single-handed war against poverty, determined to save the world. At first it had seemed to work. She had not been working, but the child needed attention and I left it to her, driving away early each day from the ramshackle house we had found to live in and coming back late. The work seemed to have its own will and its own limitless needs, eating into every moment of my time and sapping my energy like a vampire. There were big programmes to run and they needed me. I was sure this was what I had been called to do, the cause that would define my life, and so I responded willingly – naively self-important, it seemed now, looking back. There had been a lot of self in all of that expenditure of energy on behalf of the poor: self-righteousness, self-promotion, self-centredness. The only feeling I had about it now was one of embarrassment, almost shame. It had all come to seem so futile now in this empty heart of Africa. The only realities were those of war and greed and a frail daily struggle to retain the good things in human nature in the middle of so much darkness.

At the time I had not noticed any effect of this on her. Sometimes we lay in silence at night, when at an earlier stage in our marriage we would have talked and talked until we fell asleep in the early hours. Now it had become a dull routine of dropping silently, in irrelevant proximity, into exhausted oblivion.

And I still did not know. That was what was so hard to cope with now. I still did not know if any of it was true or if it was not just something my mind had concocted afterwards to make the suffering worse. All I could remember of our last conversation was something she had said about wondering if she had a fault in her nature that only allowed her to love one person properly. We had been talking about the child and I had not given her words much heed at the time, but lately they had come back to me and I had found myself wondering if there had not after all been something deep and sad in those words, a message I had missed.

# 6.

*Sunday evening*
What was the time?

I must have drifted off to sleep again. Now the canvas above my head had the opaque lightness, almost a translucent quality, that it acquired in the daytime and the heat and stuffiness were starting to build up. My head throbbed, in part from the whisky and in part from the heat and lack of fresh air. I could hear the voices of the others, deep and penetrating, coming from over the fire. They must be sitting there already, drinking instant coffee and continuing the same conversation they had started the night before, as if, like trolls frozen by the rays of the returning sun, they had not moved.

I raised myself to sit on the camp bed and took a swig of water from the plastic water bottle. Then I eased myself onto my knees and unzipped the mosquito screen. I picked up my watch and stepped out, slipping my feet into my flip-flops as I raised myself to stand and looking over the line of tents toward the fire. John and Samuel saw me at once and shouted in unison 'Good morning, Richard!' They were both grinning. I felt awkward and angry with myself. They must be thinking I had been drunk the night before and had had to sleep it off this morning. It must make me look weak in their eyes. I felt sure of that. As weak and susceptible to the temptation that might ease the hardness of this alien world as they were or had been.

I did not want that. I wanted to keep the aloofness that had given me the automatic right to take command. I had decided everything we had done so far. If I had not been there they would not have achieved anything. I was sure of that. They would have sat round the fire or at the rickety table under the tree with Simon, jotting down whatever lies he told them.

They had needed me, like a stick on their backs, to goad them into the long walks to the communities round about, where we could at least see something for ourselves and talk directly with the people we met…

Not that that had yet yielded much in the way of real, evidence-based data…

And they had known that from the beginning, known it just as Simon had. That was why this trip with Father Severino was so important – just because it was unexpected and would take us somewhere new, to a place that even Simon would not have been able to prepare in advance, where we would find something, some evidence we could use and needs that could be estimated and quantified with honesty and integrity.

Not that it would make such a vast difference in the end…People were so poor and had so very little, just as the school children had nothing more than the voices they sang with and the words of the song each morning, ringing out as though the entire sack of treasure that education was and schools might hold could be distilled down into one magic charm unfailingly recited while the mist still lay around the cattle in the cattle camps.

I waved at them and reached back inside the tent to pick up my sponge bag. Then I made my way in silence to the washing area. 'There is water already in the tank,' I heard John's voice behind me. 'Thanks,' I shouted back without turning round. It would be good to shower. The cold water would shake things clear in my mind. Then I would get dressed quickly and go back to see Father Severino and find out what time we would be leaving.

The shower was a simple contraption. A plastic water bag was hung from a tree branch against which a ladder had been leant so that you could climb up to fill the plastic bag from a bucket drawn from the well. To take a shower you stood below in the small enclosure, fenced in by corrugated iron and woven grass sheets, and opened the valve at the bottom of the water sack, unleashing a thin trickle. John and Samuel had set it up when we arrived, using the skills their years in the field had turned into second nature. I envied their ability to do these things with a resentful desire that came, I knew, from the unrequited longing to find something practical and manly in myself.

I picked up the soap and lathered myself under the flow just enough to be sure I could rinse it all off with the amount of water the bag held. The water was good and cold and it cleared my mind and brought some rationality back into my thinking. There was nothing untoward in anything this morning. I had behaved quite normally the night before and if I had got up later than usual, then it was just because I had been so worn out by the exertions of the climb up the hill the previous day. I should not read things into the situation. That would be the beginning of paranoia. It would make me like the woman I had been thinking about.

I had no clean clothes left. I always tried to cut my baggage down to a minimum on field trips, but I liked at least to change my underpants every day. This time it seemed I had got it wrong. I thrust my hand down into the depths of my rucksack like an inept Father Christmas at an old fashioned department store in a modern shopping mall trying to dig out a suitable present for an impatient child. The child was himself and so was the old man. There was nothing in-between. I was lying on my back on a sunny day by the side of the small river that meandered through a flat landscape, watching a Tiger Moth droning overhead as it practices stunts, climbing, stalling with a cough, falling, re-starting the engine with a roar. There were ladybirds on the dry stem of grass next to my eyes, yellow ones and red ones with shiny carapaces patterned with black spots.

I shook my head to clear the tangle of thoughts and images. The moments came like this and I knew it was the product of my solitude, the carapace I had retreated into without really wanting to or planning to.

I pulled on a pair of underpants I had used a few days previously. The sweat had completely dried out, so they did not feel too bad. For the rest, yesterday's bush shirt and the worn out trekking trousers I had been using all week were fine. I rolled up my sleeping bag, folded the kikoy and t-shirt I slept in and laid them out neatly on the camp bed. Then I backed out of the tent on his knees, put my socks and boots on and shambled over to join the others. There was a stiffness in my joints this morning that told me it would not be many years before I started to get old. If I had been one of the elite out here that would have been no impediment. The cattle I would have accumulated would get me a young bride, like King David, to keep me warm at night. This thought did not bother me much, except at the times when I wondered what it must be like to want someone to share your nights. It seemed incredible to think I had once taken all that for granted. So very long ago, of course.

'Hi,' I said, smiling to return the smiles that lit up the faces of John and Samuel, the way they always did when they greeted me. 'Am I late?'

'No, Richards, the women only just came,' said John. He was sitting on one of the rickety chairs that had been pulled out of the tumble-down SRRC office for their use at the table under the big smooth-trunk of the ficus tree. He seemed to have grown in stature, large and dignified like a chief seated among his courtiers to hold court. 'We were discussing the morning's news. Something interesting has happened.'

'What, don't tell me something else has cropped up to stall the talks?' I did not have to think in order to frame this question. It just came out with the spontaneity of a conditioned response. I knew it was wrong to react with this cynicism. So much was riding on the strangely mutilated peace process. People were moving. I had seen for myself the struggle of waifs and strays coming back into the south. The organisation called them IDPs – 'Internally Displaced Persons' and once it had labelled them it designed regulations for how to help them and who could do what and where and it started to count and to estimate their numbers and these had turned out to be very big. They were coming home even before the peace was signed, looking for the houses and the land they might have left behind in the small towns that no longer existed, or the cattle in the swamps they no longer knew how to tend.

I looked across the fire into the eyes of the tall, thin woman who was sitting the cooking pot that had the millet porridge that would be breakfast for the visitors. They had brought the meal with them from Kenya. The women just lit the fire, cooked and washed the dishes. This woman looked old and tired, as they always did once they had given birth a few times. I wondered how old she really was, how many children she had, what age she had been when she was married off and how many cattle had been paid for her. It always came down to women in the end when you looked for the reason why things were right or wrong in a place.

I did not know whether the people of the swamps mutilated their women. I had first found out all about it in Ethiopia and then come to realise it flowed all the way down the Nile into middle-income, tourist-friendly Egypt. In Ethiopia, of course, in some places they sewed them up.

In the dark Afar hut there was the mad old blind man with hair as white as snow lying there and calling for water in a small child's voice. He lay naked on a wooden bed calling out into the darkness of his world and down between his legs – I had noticed with a momentary revulsion – there was nothing, just a hole. They told me the man was a hundred years old. An Issa raiding party had caught him when he was a child tending his father's camels out in the black, volcanic moonscape of the Danakil, and had cut his penis off. He called out over and over again, his voice hardly more than a hopeless, droning moan. Then a girl had appeared in the doorway, young and beautiful with the delicate,
regular features and large, expressive eyes of the women of the Horn, her neck and arms adorned with beads, bracelets, heavy chunks of metal in the Afar way. She was carrying a water gourd. She offered it to the old man in silence and after he had guzzled some water, as she turned to leave, she smiled and I could see that all her were teeth filed to sharp triangular points like a saw.

'Hey, Richards, wake up! You need a coffee!' Samuel was speaking to me along the tunnel that connected me with the present. 'You must have had a lot to drink last night with the Father!'

'Oh! Yeah, yeah, I certainly did!' I laughed back and took the mug that Samuel was holding out.

'There is no sugar left,' said Samuel. 'But you do not take sugar.'

'That's right.' Normally I would have been angry and frustrated at their inability to ration themselves and make their supplies last. But today it did not seem to matter. I was wearing dirty underpants, so who was I to talk?

'Tell me what the news is, John,' I said. 'Now I am properly awake.'

'There is trouble in Upper Nile,' said John. 'There has been fighting'

'Who against who?'

'It is not sure. There are different stories.'

'It is never certain in Upper Nile, though, is it? There are so many different groups. I can never understand who is on the Government's side and who is just out for themselves.'

I could have said something about Evans Pritchard and about the hierarchically ordered anarchy his studies of kinship among the Nuer had somehow sifted out of all the raiding and fighting, a system of overlapping allegiances that would have defeated any attempt to impose political order or stability beyond the ebb and flow of the seasons and the cattle raids that came and went with them. I could have said all that, or something to that effect, and I would just have made myself ridiculous, like a jumped up little professor far away from his classroom. Or, worse than that, I would have just sounded patronising, a silly little white man far away from home, out of his depth in the swamp.
But I could not stop myself from thinking along those lines. That was what divided me from these people. I could sympathise with them and like them as friends and colleagues, but I could not keep myself from seeing the world the way I did. I could only be silent and tactful, when I remembered to hold my tongue.

'Dr. Melchior is there,' said Samuel with a grin. 'He is trying to make peace.'

'I thought he had missed the boat on the peace process.'

'He is there.'

'Will he join the leadership, though?'

'He is not at all the talks, he is in Upper Nile. That is his choice. Maybe he is building his position there. Maybe he is making peace.'

'But where was this fighting? What exactly happened?'

'There was an attack on an oil camp. The government may retaliate. There is a lot of confusion. Nobody is exactly sure of the details. They did not say much. It was just a short message from Loki to alert field workers in Upper Nile. They will evacuate some places. All far from here, don't worry.'

I sat down next to Daniel on the tree trunk by the fire. I sipped my coffee and then I said 'I'll go check with Father Severino about today just as soon as I finish this. Are you guys all ready?'

'Yes,' said John. 'We are just waiting for Simon to come with the SRRC permit.'

'Permit?'

'Yes, Richard. You know we need that in order to travel.'

'He's not going to block us is he? I mean because of his fighting?'

'Don't worry, Simon is coming with us. It is a formality.'

I heard the words and saw the smile on John's face. I wanted to be reassured, but I was not. There was a tightness in my stomach that had started from the moment the possibility of making this journey had arisen, like the rain that stopped the planes from landing. I could not convince myself that we would be able to get into the vehicle and drive out of this place. The horror of the prison cell was growing in this feeling, this claustrophobia that took me outside any rational consideration of my circumstances. For whatever reason I had to get out into the landscape, away from the hopeless camp under the big tree and the pointless circular conversations. I knew I would not breath freely until we were safely down the track several kilometres with a new horizon ahead of us.

'I hope you are right,' I said, trying to sound calm.

'Do not worry. He will be here at any moment. Now our breakfast is made, so let us pray.'

I joined the others in bowing my head as John offered up a long string of supplications and blessings in the evangelical style. He had a natural authority as he led the prayers. His physical stature and the deep, rich melody of his voice gave him this without effort. The hesitancy of the past few days was behind him, it seemed, now that the pointless complexity of the survey was all but done and I felt that my own authority was waning in equal proportion to the growth of this other's. They had needed me to guide them through the tortuous form-filling and a self-driven belief in getting beyond it, to reach a truth that would ultimately convert itself into the substance of our labours, had fuelled the energy of leadership that I had found inside myself, so that it had seemed natural for me to drive and goad them into the long forced marches carrying their participatory assessment beans and folders full of forms to fill in, like the missionaries of a bygone era with their Bibles and magic lantern slides. Now it had melted half away and I retained only the desperate, obsessive longing for the trip to the Jiye village which had been promised. My remaining willpower was focused on getting my way on this and force of habit unsettled me with the suspicion that the others, led by Simon, would try to sabotage it, not out of malice, but simply because they were lazy and could not see the point in travelling so far to see something they could simply imagine. Poverty was everywhere and its face was predictable.

But I would have my way. I no longer had any desire to lead the team. I did not see the team, only the journey that I had to make. They were apart from me. At root that was how it had always been anyway.

John finished the prayers and said a loud and very final 'Amen'. The women started to fill the metal bowls with uji. The gate swung open and, like a predatory beast that comes boldly into the firelight from its wandering across the empty plains, drawn from far away by the faint scent it has caught, and makes a beeline for the carcass, Simon entered.

'So,' he said in a loud, cheerful voice. 'Everyone is ready!'

The Sudanese greeted him warmly with handshakes and invited him to sit down and eat a bowl of uji with them. He took it from the woman and sat down on the chair which John had vacated. Meanwhile one of the other women came out from the kitchen, as though obeying an order transmitted telepathically, and went silently over to the office, from where she brought another chair that she placed behind John, who immediately sat down without saying anything to her.

The Sudanese ate rapidly in silence until their bowls were empty and they were all sitting back with a second cup of instant coffee in their hands. 'So' said John to Simon, 'You have heard the news this morning?'

'Which news are you talking of, brother?' Simon smiled his usual smile, full of suggestion, as thought he knew full well what John was alluding to, but wished to play a game with him, slowly teasing out of him whatever information he might possesses without in return revealing anything.

'You know what I am referring to I think,' said John. His voice still had the ponderous quality that came into it when he led the prayers before meals. Simon seemed to shrink slightly, as though acknowledging an authority, but this was only for a moment. He recovered his equilibrium at once and laughed.

'Come, ' he said, 'Your radio must have told you something. I should use it now to contact our headquarters.'

'There has been a raid,' said John, as confused and slow as usual once more.

'It's a long way from here!' I could not keep myself from blurting out these words in a tone that betrayed the anxiety that was filling my mind.

'Yes,' said Simon slowly, hissing the sibilant like air coming out of a tyre valve. 'A long way. I do not think you should worry, my friend. I know you are anxious. Perhaps you are frightened?' He laughed. 'Do not worry, we shall be very fine today!'

I felt the blood rush to my cheeks. I had never imagined my anxiety might be interpreted as fear of possible danger. I could see now why I had sensed the slipping away of my authority. They thought I was frightened, an inexperienced, greenhorn coward from headquarters who feared he might find himself out of his depth in a place where danger could come upon us.

How could this grotesque misinterpretation have come about? Could they not see that, on the contrary, I was desperate to make this journey and had only been worried that some excuse might be found to delay or prevent it? Could they not see that? – that I was so driven by the need to find what lay at the heart of my world of suffering in order to justify everything else we did, the planes, the tents, the food, the missions and the money?

It felt like a trap. If I were to start to explain all this I would only make myself look foolish. They would assume I was trying to justify myself after the event, in response to the accusations, and was re-interpreting the reality in order to suit this purpose. The inside of my mind was so far away from anyone else, it seemed. Except perhaps Father Severino.

I felt a need to see the priest right away. I should go at once to make sure all was well and the vehicle prepared for our departure. Time was ticking by, time my enemy out here, time which they, my colleagues, did not respect or respond to, but which seemed to expand for them to the shape they needed, while cramping and restricting me, by contrast, into days too short to achieve half of the long list I had of things that must be done.

'Today will be a good day for our journey,' said Simon. 'It will be good to make a check of this Jiye village. Very useful, very useful. Our statistics need to be completed and then you need to increase our food aid allocation to accommodate them.' He smiled round at the group, apparently pleased at having revealed his motivation for endorsing the trip with so much enthusiasm.

'It will be interesting,' said John. 'I do not know the Jiye.'

'They are like the Toposa,' said Samuel.

'Masai, Turkana, Toposa, Jiye, all are brothers,' said Daniel, suddenly speaking for the first time. 'I have seen the Jiye and the Toposa when I am organising food drops. They all look similar.'

'But they fight each other all the time, they kill each other, they hate!' Simon laughed. 'They are difficult, dangerous people.'

'They fight because they are so similar!' said Samuel and the others laughed too, as though he had cracked a joke.

'They fight because of cattle,' said John.

'Just like the Dinka and the Nuer, like the Murle, like your people,' I said, 'and they do the same dances, don't they? You are all the same really.' I was aware of my own viciousness, as I spoke, like someone taking a joke too far. It was my revenge attack. I was serving them for the brand of cowardice that had been placed on me. My anger was small and mean and I knew it would have been better to keep it to myself. But the words were out before I could apply reason to control my lips.

'Yes, Richards,' said John slowly. 'All the fighting is for cattle.'

'It was that way before the oil,' said Samuel.

'It was that way before the Arabs,' I said. The anger that had made me lash out in a small and vicious way was gone. My words had sounded like scorn, deep-seated and racial. But they were not. I knew that and surely they must also see it. They had embarrassed me and made me feel small and I had struck back blindly, grabbing the first weapon that came to hand and lashing out with it. It had been nothing more than that, a blind lashing out. I looked around at their faces, smiling, to show I had not meant anything by my words.

Simon stood up. 'It was that way before the British,' he said, looking directly at me through his dark glasses, challenging me to make the next move in a duel that had not yet been formalised.

I stood up too and stepped back from the fire. 'I must go and check that Father Severino is ready, ' I said.

'Come' said John to Simon. 'While Richards is gone I will radio Loki for more news.'

'We should talk to Rumbek,' said Simon.

'We will try.'

I shambled down the track like a penitent. My colleagues were professionals who knew what they were doing and knew the world in which they operated with all its limitations and possibilities. It was their world and their self-confidence within its confines had no necessary limits. My ability to impose myself came only with the unworkable systems I brought with me, the very systems I was railing against, knowing how useless they were. But without them I was nothing. They had no use for me. I was an amateur, contrite, humble and insincere. I was full of resentment.

I pushed the high gate opened and saw at once that the few necessary preparations were underway. The Landcruiser was parked in front of the house, from where Father Severino was emerging, dressed in a t-shirt and jeans and carrying a large cardboard box, which he took to the back of the vehicle and stowed inside. I went over to him.

'Good morning, Father,' I said, shaking hands. 'I wanted to thank you for last night.'
Then, before the priest could reply, I added 'Can I help?'

I did not want to talk about the conversation we had shared in the shadowy light of the paraffin lantern. It was part of my self-disgust, part of my weakness, self-doubt and self-pity and it would not do. I hated myself, just as I resented my colleagues. In the presence of the priest I felt only shame.

Father Severino looked directly into my eyes. We were the same height so that there was no looking up or down in this. 'Yes, we have some things to take with us to the community,' he said. 'You can help me bring them from the house.' He paused, still looking directly into my eyes, so that I was immediately conscious of something almost profound, a sensitivity to the self-emasculation that must surely always permeate the degradation of the confessional. Then, with a slight gesture of his head, he added 'And thank you for coming last night. Our conversation was interesting.'

Just inside the front door of the house there was a pile of cardboard boxes identical to the first. I picked one up and carried it out to the vehicle. Father Severino followed.

We made two round-trips without speaking. Then I said 'Actually, I wanted to apologise.' I found I wanted to say sorry – I could see this now as we carried the boxes and the clear light of the sun shone down, hard and bright, directly onto us – so that the incident could be closed off and the day move forward without reference to it.

'The boxes contain some food items' said Father Severino, 'for the women with babies, you know, and some medical supplies. Sister Lucy runs a clinic whenever we go – just basic healthcare, especially for the pregnant women and the young mothers with their babies. We need the WHO to come and vaccinate.'

'Father, I want to apologise,' I said again.

'The priest put the box he was carrying down inside the vehicle then turned to face me. 'Apologise?' he asked. 'Apologise for what? We had a good evening. We discussed many things and came to know one another. To me that seems a reason for rejoicing, not for an apology.'

'I was rude to you and I was boring, talking about myself, stupid stuff. Because of the alcohol, you know…'

'I did not feel that. I thought we talked about important things, deep things that matter.'

'But I felt bad afterwards and this morning I felt worse. I felt I must have insulted you. I was even starting to wonder whether you might be going to tell me I was no longer welcome on this trip.'

'No no no!' Father Severino raised his voice emphatically. He did not laugh, but he smiled and there was a warmth in his smile that must surely immediately remove the challenges and the barriers that define relationships between people. 'Richards,' he said. 'I was glad of your presence and your company. I was glad to have you to talk to about these things, because they matter to you and you did not hide them from me. And in this place I do not find so many people to talk to in this way. I could talk about myself a lot too and perhaps I needed that. No, Richards, I was happy last night. I think probably I had been waiting for the chance to talk this way for a long time. Maybe too long…'

We continued loading up the Landcruiser. When we had finished, Father Severino turned towards me and took hold of my arm firmly so that our eyes met and held each other in momentary communion.

'Richards,' he said, 'you are asking many questions. You cannot accept the world, because everything you see is tainted with something you want to fight and you cannot respond to God, because he is not there. So you ask questions and you do not find answers and it makes you unhappy and it makes you alone.

'I do not have answers for the questions you are asking. My faith is blind. I respond to it without asking questions. That is what I am called to, not to question.

'But I have told you from the first that I know your questions mean you are good. There is something in you that can offer so much. And so much is needed. That is why I know you will enjoy this trip. You will see these people and you will find you can do something. Maybe that will give you an answer. That is all I can say.'

He relaxed his grip and grinned, turning to look a final time at the veranda where the boxes had been. 'Now I think we are ready. I will go and find Sister Lucy. How about your friends? Are they going to come?'

'Yes, they are. They're all waiting at the SRRC compound, including Simon.'

Father Severino went into the house to find Sister Lucy, leaving me standing by the front passenger door of the Landcruiser. I guessed Sister Lucy would occupy the front seat. Since she was the only woman letting her have that seat would be the best way to deal with any requirements of propriety. It would be her accustomed place, in any case. I felt calm now inside. I had not know how things would be between myself and the priest, but my usual feeling of guilt after drinking hard and emptying the emotional dustbin had convinced me that things would at best be awkward. I had no reason to doubt the priest. There was no way such a man would not mean what he said. That was the essential thing that had drawn me, was it not? The feeling that you could trust him even to the point where you spoke about the things that usually stayed inside. So now it was good and calm and all was well. I was not despicable in the way I had started the day feeling that I was. The trip was on and everyone was on board. All was well.

And yet it was not. Inside it was still rotten. I knew what I really thought and what I perceived when I looked around in there. The interpretation that Father Severino put on things was a reflection of his own goodness and his strength. He could not see the rottenness, just as he did not have answers to the questions.

'Come on then!' Father Severino emerged from the house, followed by Sister Lucy, who locked the door. The priest smiled and strode round to the driver's door with big, energetic steps. He looked well and young. 'It is good to be going somewhere, isn't it?' he said. 'I always feel excited at this moment, just when we are leaving.'

'Yes,' I said, agreeing without thinking, and then added a greeting to Sister Lucy, who was getting into the front seat in the slow, clumsy way of the over-weight.

'Good morning,' she said, smiling. 'You don't mind me sitting here at the front and leaving you men at the back?'

I smiled back. Father Severino turned the key in the ignition. He warmed the engine for a few minutes and then put the Landcruiser into gear, releasing the clutch with a smoothness that only came when you had driven a lot in the bush. We set off through the gateway. Behind us the compound guard, emerging silently from the shadows of the trees, swung the door shut.

## 7.

*Sunday later in the day*
They were still sitting in a circle around the smouldering embers of the fire, drinking instant coffee and talking. Always talking – sitting in a circle and talking. When I had taken the big man from New York to meet John Garang at New Site, we had been kept waiting for hours sitting around a wooden table because the elders were busy talking, sitting in a circle and talking, and they would not interrupt their talk at any outsider's bidding, no matter how high and mighty he might be, how far he might have come, how tight his schedule. It must continue until its course was run. That was the way things should be out here in the endless flat grasslands, where every device, every gadget, every trapping the world had to offer had been chewed up and rejected. The few roads fell rapidly into disrepair, the termites consumed the buildings, there was nowhere close-by where electricity might be generated and then distributed, the Jonglei canal lay empty, like a miniature rift valley below the few passing light aircraft on their lonely quest for the network of sandy landing strips dotted across the grasslands, amphibious oil exploration vehicles lay rusting in the deepest swamps; I had even seen the rusting hulk of a tank half-buried in the sand half-way across a river in Bahr el Ghazal, the abandoned detritus of some long forgotten battle. The elephant grass grew tall, high above a man's head and waved in the breeze, the clouds floated across the sky and unleashed the deluge that every year turned the grassland into swamp. The river spread itself into an endless shimmering lake with reed beds where the white egrets and grey herons perched and flew on silent wings from one isolated palm tree to another. The villages became islands and the women poled long, narrow canoes to distant, hidden markets. The cattle roamed from cattle camp to cattle camp, following the grazing. The men raided one another's cattle camps to steal the cattle and bought their

brides with the cattle they had taken and then they sat around the fire and talked. The only things that had come easily here were the instruments of modern death, the guns that had so quickly finished off the wild animals – the elephants and giraffes and lions – and were now so easily applied to the hunting down of men.

I went directly over to my tent and pulled out my rucksack. I laid it down on the hard ground and began to fill it carefully with the equipment I always carried, the individually wrapped and labelled contents of the survival kit, together with a spare pair of underpants and t-shirt, unwashed but at least dried out from the sweat of several days, in case we had to overnight for some reason or the sweat became too uncomfortable round my chest and the small of my back and in my crotch, my torch for the pitch-black night and the Chinese medicine for malaria, even though it seemed scarcely relevant for such a short trip. Inside I knew that that was not the point. This was a ritual, like a knight putting on his armour before a battle. Everything had to be there in the right order or my luck might fail.

'Packing up your toys, eh, Richard?' Simon's voice was very close behind me. I had not heard him approach and it took me by surprise. His tone was amused and at the same time oily, the way it always was, as though even while he was constantly mocking the futility of everything I did in conformity with the rules and guidelines that came from outside and had so little to do with the way things were in reality, at the same time he was trying to ingratiate himself, weedling like a self-appointed tour-guide trying to talk up his tip. 'When you leave, you will leave these things for me?' he said. 'They will be useful for me and you can get new ones in Nairobi.'

The loathing I felt towards him was like a bad taste in my mouth. What I saw as his self-serving cynicism was the heart of a termite army that was eating away and undermining the foundations of the entire elaborate edifice I had built in order to justify the things I did and the life I led. Another man would have reacted with anger or with scorn now, coldly choosing harsh words with which to demean his tormentor and put him in his place, or else would have just let the anger come out in whatever words it chose, without regret, and a hierarchy would have been established which both men would have understood and had to accept, like dogs in a pack. But for me always the self-doubt drove me down into myself so that all I wished was to be rid of this pest that hovered like a mosquito that cannot be caught or killed keeping me from the reflections and the rituals that defined this part of the day. 'Yes, alright,' I said quietly without looking round. 'When I go, you can have my toys.'

I did up the cord and fastened the straps on the rucksack. Simon smiled and, darting forward suddenly, picked it up off the ground. 'Let me take it to the vehicle, 'he said.
'You are getting old.'

'Yes, I feel old,' I replied, smiling mechanically in reply. 'Old and tired.'

Simon laughed and loped, half-running, over to the Landcruiser. 'Richards is feeling old,' he shouted to the others, who were now gathered there talking to Sister Lucy through the open window. Father Severino was not there.

'Oh, so you are getting old, Richards,' laughed Samuel, 'You are becoming an elder, then!.

'So you must have the best seat,' added John. 'We must respect you!'

'You'll have to give me a stick as well, a fine ebony cane, like the one they gave me in Mabaan county. And I'll need some cattle!'

'And a wife!' shouted Simon, excited with the humour he had initiated.

'Yes a wife,' said John. 'You need a wife. Then you will feel young again!'

'Perhaps,' I said, smiling. 'But I need cattle first or I'll never get one.'

They all laughed at this and got into the vehicle. I sat on the back seat behind Sister Lucy, next to Simon and John. Samuel and Daniel and the two guards crammed themselves into the back with the boxes.

The corrugated iron door of the long-drop toilet swung open and Father Severino emerged. He poured some water over his hands from the plastic jug by the well and came over to us. 'All ready?' he asked. 'Then let us go with the blessing of the Almighty,'

'Amen,' said Sister Lucy, crossing herself. Father Severino paused a moment in silent prayer. Then he too crossed himself, started the engine and eased the heavily loaded vehicle forward and out through the gate.

The track down past the shabby, unkempt huts on the edge of the village to the landing strip was familiar. It skirted the side of the wide open space that had been cleared by hand and then turned sharply towards the south. The air-conditioning was broken so we had the windows open, which allowed some of the breeze generated as soon as we started to move to sweep through the cabin, but we were already cooked and perspiring inside and the relief at slow speed was only slight. There was no shade, just an endless sea of grass –tall, silver grass out of which widely-spaced acacia trees protruded on all side, always just beyond reach. Further away small hills, already hazy in the late morning heat, stuck straight out of the ground like warts and boils on the smooth skin of a human face.

Father Severino drove slowly along the rough track, avoiding pot-holes. 'We are carrying a lot of weigh,' he said, 'and the new brakes have not been tested.'

'At least the land is flat,' I said. With the windows open we had to shout above the diesel throb of the engine.

'The bumps take it out on the suspension, anyway, especially when we are heavy. Already I had to weld the place where it is attached down here,' – he pointed toward the wheel housing at his feet. 'I do not know how it is called in English…'

He drove on in silence for a while and then seemed to find his sense of the vehicle's load and weight and reactions that he had been looking for. He took one hand off the steering wheel, resting his elbow on the open window and shouted over his head 'So tell me what the news is, Simon? It is so long since I have heard anything. They must keep you up to date.'

No-one answered. John looked round at Samuel and then both of them turned to look at Simon. Daniel was already asleep at the back, lying down on the lateral bench at one side, completely out of sight behind the boxes piled up in the middle. Simon continued to sit in silence. His dark glasses made it impossible to see his eyes.

I wondered if he too had fallen asleep in the stuffy heat. I decided to answer the question with what I knew. It might get the others started onto something new. 'There's been some fighting,' I said.

'Oh,' said Father Severino. 'Where? Nearby?'

'No, Father, somewhere to the north, in Upper Nile. Dr. Melchior's men are involved, I think.' I spoke rapidly, wanting to reassure the priest that his could not affect our journey. It was far away, almost irrelevant to us, like the background noise on the radio that brought the news. I looked round at the others, seeking confirmation. 'Did they say anything on the radio this morning John? You were going to ask with Simon…'

John looked at Simon again. It was always like this whenever the conversation turned to news of what was happening now, especially when the news was of fighting. The SPLA was touchy, of course. They had banned the carrying of GPS's by aid personnel and at times seemed to resent the presence of any form of radio communications. In the early days of the operations the SPLA had been convinced that unguarded talk over the radio about military dispositions had been monitored by Sudan government forces and their spies and had led to one or two devastating attacks on unprepared SPLA units. Now there were strict rules about the subjects that could be discussed over the airwaves – the daily weather report, state of the runway, logistics, health, emergencies, flight schedules, nothing more. Yet everyone knew that the Sudanese themselves used the radios for much more than this, talking to one another in Dinka and Nuer, discussing politics and news. There was a fine line which they seemed to understand imperfectly between what would be acceptable and what would not and the rebel officials were complicit in this when it suited them and were often part of it.

I was sure that that was what was going on here. Simon must have been with them chatting over the radio, I was sure. Now the men were obviously uncertain about where they stood. They looked to Simon to take the lead and he was holding back because he knew it was the best way to maintain the power his position gave him. As long as no-one other than he knew precisely where the line was drawn, he was in command, representing a hidden but all pervading authority in the heartland of its own territory far from all the other organisations that came here with their planes and people and food and medicines. They only came on his sufferance. The wrong gesture or even the wrong word could bring that to an end.

So Simon said nothing. John looked across, past Simon's face hidden behind its dark glasses, at me.

And I found no words in response to this silent query. I would still have liked to break the secret tyranny, to assert the fact that I was the leader of this team and that we represented something bigger and richer and finer than Simon and the half-baked, vicious mafia that was all his lot were at root, but I also knew that these thoughts were not wholly honest or fair. The silence hung heavy between us in the drowsy heat.

Then at last John spoke, choosing his words slowly. 'No, nothing is known,' he said. 'It is always like this in Upper Nile, very unstable.'

'Yes, don't worry, Richards!' said Simon, suddenly alive, grinning broadly beneath his dark glasses.' It is very far from here.'

He leaned forward and tapped the priest on the shoulder in a familiar way. 'Richards was worried, Father, that the fighting might affect us, but we told him he should not be afraid when he is with us. The SRRC will not allow anything bad to happen to an important official like him!' He laughed and the others laughed with him, uneasily, as thought sensing that this joke had been overplayed and was going to turn sour at any moment.

'Richards is right,' said Father Severino, turning briefly to look at Simon across his left shoulder. It was a hard, serious look that did not invite further humour. 'It would have been a great pity if this trip had to be cancelled. Just think of the people where we are going. They are waiting for us and they need our help. If security had cancelled this trip it would have been very sad and very serious for them. Don't you agree, Simon?'

Simon said nothing in reply.

We drove on in silence for a few minutes. Then Father Severino asked 'Who is this Doctor Melchior? Is he important? One of the leaders?'

Again there was silence and again I felt obliged to fill the awkward void that was opening up. 'He was one of the leaders,' I said. 'And he wants to be one again, like they all do…' I checked himself, realising that I had never bothered to ascertain where Simon might stand in all of this. He was a Murle, not a Nuer or a Dinka. Where did the Murles line themselves up? Who had they gone along with in all the intrigues and the in-fighting and changing of sides?

'He was a minister at one time,' said John.

'You mean on the other side?' asked Father Severino.

'Yes,' said John. 'History is complicated especially in South Sudan.'

'But before that he was one of the leaders, wasn't he?' I said. 'Of the rebels, I mean.' Now that John had spoken more freely it seemed I could talk about these things without breaking some unspoken taboo.

'Yes, he was,' said John. 'Before the massacre...' A sudden bitterness entered his voice, as though for the first time during the entire mission something had touched a raw spot within him, where issues that truly mattered to him were in play.

'The Nuers are complicated people, Richards,' said Simon. 'You should know that from those big books you are reading every night in your tent...'

'Which books are those?' asked Father Severino.

'Evans Pritchard. You may have heard of him. Came up with the world's first in-depth study of kinship systems...Spent a lot of time living in a tent with the Nuer. In fact he was paid to do it by the British administration when they ran out of ideas about how to try to control the Nuer. Someone came up with the idea they should try to understand them, instead of bombing them and gassing them, so they brought Evan Pritchard in. He was already working with the Bantu tribes down on the Congo border.' I delivered this information in a loud clear voice, making sure Simon could hear every word, challenging him to say something stupid about it.

'Really?' said Father Severino. 'There are so many books, but this one must be interesting. Maybe I should read it, though I have not worked with the Nuer.'

'Difficult people,' said Simon.

'And this Dr. Melchior is out there with an army and he is causing trouble – fighting?' asked Father Severino.

'Maybe,' said Simon. 'Who can tell in the swamps? Sometimes there are stories of a massacre or an attack and it is just people moving their cows to follow the rain.'

'But they are far away,' said John. 'It does not concern us here.'

'Everything should concern us,' said Father Severino, as though he were choosing to contradict in order to make a point.

'I mean it will not reach us,' said John.

'Let us pray that that is so,' said Sister Lucy, turning round suddenly to face the men seated behind her. 'Many terrible things have happened and they can happen again. We should pray to the Lord to deliver us at all times.'

John and Samuel replied to this with an 'Amen' that came out in an accidental unison that was almost comic, or at least that is the way it seemed to the sniggering schoolboy inside me.

…..

The day went by. I gazed out at the unchanging landscape. The sea of grass stretched to the horizon. The hills and mountains were fainter now, scarcely discernible in the intense, throbbing heat haze. It was some time since we had left the main road to Torit along what looked like no more that a cattle track that meandered through the bush, avoiding trees and shrubs, merging here and there with other tracks. 'It would be difficult to drive here at night,' I said.

'I have never tried at night,' said Father Severino, 'but I am sure you are right.'

'How long till we get to the village?' I asked. 'I mean how much time will we have there before we have to return?'

'I am not sure if we will return,' said the priest. 'Today, I mean. We have been driving very slowly. Perhaps we should stay the night there. We shall see.'

I looked round at the other passengers. The men sitting next to me and at the back were sleeping as far as I could tell. In front of me Sister Lucy had snuggled sideways against the back of her seat in an attitude that suggested the she too was asleep.

'How are you doing, Father?' I asked. 'Do you need some help with the driving? Everyone else is sleeping. Maybe you feel sleepy too?'

'I am alright, Richards,' said Father Severino. 'I am used to these journeys. But I am worried about the Landcruiser. It is getting old. I have no spare parts left. The shock absorbers should be changed after this trip and it is past the time to change the oil and the oil filter. Like this it cannot last much longer.'

'Is it ok now? I mean the engine sounds pretty normal, doesn't it?' I did not know anything much, but the staccato growl was the same I had heard in a thousand four-wheel drive diesels like this one.

'It is fine for now and we will soon arrive,' said the priest. 'I did not mean to alarm you. I was just thinking out loud. I do that sometimes when I have a lot of things on my mind.'

'And you must have a lot on your mind today.'

'Yes, I suppose I do,' said the priest, not turning as he spoke, for we had begun to descend very slowly into a dried out river-bed and he needed to concentrate in order to pick the best route among the ruts and boulders. 'To being with I have the responsibility of you and your friends.'

'I am sorry, Father. I wish I could have come alone. Then it would only be one person.'

'Don't worry. I am glad they have come. I want them to see this place, especially Simon. He is the boss around here you know, so I need him to help me. If he wants he can do a lot. Besides he has brought his bodyguards with him, so we should be safer than ever.'

I looked at the man sitting next to me with his head drooping forward in awkward slumber. 'Yes,' I said. I leaned forward so that I could talk quietly into Father Severino's ear. 'He is in a position of power and it will be more so when the peace comes. What's more, he knows it. He's already setting himself up to be the local dictator around here and to take all he can. The aid he gets now, especially the food drops – that's a base for power, you know. That's all they see. They control a resource and it gives them power.'

'Richards, you are too cynical. You have to believe that something good is happening in all of this. You have to see the humanity in other people. It is not all bad. It is not all exploitation.'

'What about you and the bishop, then? Isn't that the same? Or pretty similar anyway?'

Father Severino frowned and said nothing for several minutes. Then he nodded slowly. 'Yes, it is,' he said. 'People are weak and ambitious. We all are. But we can also all be good to one another. We are not only the bad side of ourselves.'

'Father, it is easy to believe in the poor and the fight for social justice and an end to misery and poverty. Even pop stars can do that. I used to be like that. I was so fired up I could not sleep at night. The issues burnt into my brain, images of people suffering, starving children, mutilated war victims, child prostitutes. That is all my life was and it took me over like a fever…That was before.'

'Yes, you told me this last night, you know, although not in these words. And 'before' means before your wife died, I know. And when she died everything changed and the world seemed only bad.'

'No, Father, before…I was so wrapped up in the work I was doing that I think I lost her before that. I was arrogant and I thought I was important – going to achieve something. I thing she knew better. She could see through all of that and I don't think she liked what she saw. In fact I'm not sure she still loved me at all at the end… But I'll never know that now…'

The priest said something in reply. His eyes were firmly fixed on the track in front of him as he shifted down to low-box and eased the vehicle up and out of the water-course, threading his way between ruts grown too deep and boulders that might shatter an oil sump or a differential. Then, as he manoeuvred over the lip and back onto the level, he took one hand off the wheel and pointed straight ahead with a cry that was tinged with jubilation: 'Look! There is the village!'

We had travelled for several hours without stopping and I judged we must have covered something between forty and sixty miles. It might as well have been a hundred. I had not checked the odometer and it was always difficult to tell when you were moving slowly through the bush. You wanted the distance you covered to be bigger than it usually turned out to be, as though inside the archetypal image of burning up the miles down an empty four-lane motorway had programmed your expectations. The landscape had changed imperceptible as they went long, but now it was rougher and drier. The grass was less luxuriant too, low and patchy with open areas of gravelly waste, like the desert around Loki with which this land was one.

I looked forwards through the windscreen without being able to see anything special at first. Then, after a minute or two, I saw what looked like huts - round bee-hive shapes, made out of dried elephant grass that trailed in long, untidy strands down to the ground. They were the same hard dry colour as the sandy earth that surrounded them, which was what made it so hard to discern them from a distance. 'Yes,' I said quietly. 'I can see it now.' Inside I felt an easing of tension, as though this journey's end was its whole purpose, the end of a race. Then I added 'I guess we should wake the others?'

Father Severino chuckled quietly. 'No need,' he said. 'They will wake when we stop moving. People always do. Have you not ever noticed that?'

## 8.

*Sunday night*

Father Severino revved the engine hard with the bravado that surges for the moment at the end of a long day's journey through a lonely landscape. Then he accelerated along what had become a broad, dusty track towards the village that was coming into view ahead.

The huts were packed closely together, almost touching one another, small round cells of rough, coarse thatch, each one like a messy, shaggy head of hair capped by the protruding head of the center pole, around which a garland of dried maize cobs was tied. On the front side of each one a low doorway reached only to hip-height. To go inside you would have to get down on your knees.

We parked in the patchy shade of a dusty acacia tree some fifty yards short of the tube well that marked the gateway to the village. I jumped out quickly and made for a quiet spot the other side of the tree. My bladder felt so distended that it would explode like a balloon filled with water at the slightest touch to my lower abdomen. It was always like that - far worse in the planes, of course, because they had no toilet facilities and once you had taken off you were committed to a minimum of four hours flight out of Loki, depending on where you were going. I had never had the self-discipline to forego a cup of coffee or tea in the canteen in the pre-dawn darkness before taking the plane into the field and I always paid for it with hours of growing misery that ended with a desperate, ignominious, shuffling dash to the end of the landing strip where I could relieve myself, nearly always under the gaze of a group of school children come to watch the plane land, or my colleagues still seated on board and waiting for me to join them for the onward trip.

The hot urine flowed out, burning its way through tissue, and the pain I had experienced on every one of those previous occasions came into my mind with the immediacy of a loud film trailer in the darkened cinema of my tightly closed, screwed up eyes.

I had always had this weakness, I reminded myself in a mental note that never failed to repeat itself, ever since I could remember. This was not an old man thing, despite my half-meant joking with Simon and the others in the morning. I had always had a weak bladder. My mother had talked about it when I made them stop on long car journeys to holiday cottages and grudging visits to forgotten northern grandparents. And my wife used to joke about it every time I had to stop the Landover almost as soon as we had cleared the straggling ribbon development slums at the edge of Addis and were heading for the Rift.

I zipped up my fly and turned back to join the others. I could hear their voices as they yawned and stretched, asked what time it was, struggled, half-asleep and clumsy, out of the Landcruiser and slammed the doors shut.

Father Severino was talking to Simon and John. He moved around as he spoke, active and energetic, as though the long drive far from tiring him had roused him to a new day. He opened the back doors of the Landcruiser wide and looked at the supplies we had brought. 'I'll get some of the men to carry the boxes over later,' he said. 'First we must go and meet our friends. Then I will show you around.'

'It is already late," I heard Simon's sharp, incisive voice. 'We will not have much time.'

I hurried back over. My first thought was that even now, after coming all the way down the road, Simon was going to try to sabotage the mission. I yielded to a sudden surge of anger that came out in a shout: 'If we are short of time, that's because of you, all of you!'

I reached where they were standing, still shouting despite the diminished distance between us. 'Every day it is the same. We should be up early, working while it is still cool, but you stay lazing around in your tents until the sun is already hot and then you sit around and talk while the women do all the work, washing your dishes and making your breakfast. Always the same! Always late! Always half the day wasted before it's gone and we always end up working in the hottest time of the day!'

No-one said anything in reply. The men just stood and looked at one another. John and Samuel were both smiling in an awkward, embarrassed way, wanting to be conciliatory, but not sure enough about what was going on to know if they should intervene.

The silence grew distended, like a droplet of sweat in the heavy air, until it was ruptured by a loud laugh, raucous and forced, from Simon. 'Hey, Richards!' he said. 'Maybe you are still asleep and you are dreaming! Wake up, my friend! We are already, where you wanted to be. And nobody has attacked us, no militia, no Doctor Melchior, ha ha! You should be happy!'

'I know we are here!' I said, gaining some control over myself. I knew that any further show of anger would gain nothing and would only turn me into a clown. 'We have just arrived and already you are talking about leaving, even before we begin to do anything.'

Simon smiled. 'I was only mentioning the time,' he said, holding out his wrist to show the large digital sports watch he wore. 'You can see the time. We should not travel in the dark. It is against the OLS rules.'

'So why did we start so late?' I persisted.

'But Richards,' Simon's laughter seemed genuine now. "It was you who woke up late this morning! Your head was not so good, I think! Isn't that so?' He turned to the others with gesture of his hands to solicit their concurrence. In return they laughed. The laughter was good humored. I could tell they wanted to defuse the situation and I knew I should go along with that for the sake of the common good. Whatever that might mean…

Father Severino had left us in the meantime and gone round to open the bonnet and take a look at the engine. "It will cool down here," he said. "It will have a good rest!'

'Father,' I said. I wanted to draw him into the debate on my side, as though there was argument to win. 'We will not leave before we have done everything, will we? I mean before you have finished your work and we have seen all that you wanted to show us?'

'I think we will camp tonight,' said Father Severino. 'Then there will not be a problem and we can drive back safely tomorrow. 'We have two tents and three people can sleep in the Landcruiser.'

'Then we need to radio security,' said John.

'And we do not have a radio,' added Samuel.

'No need to worry,' said Simon. 'Richards is a big man. He can break the rules and there will not be a problem.' He fixed his cunning eyes on mine as his habitual grin spread wider into a sarcastic leer that matched the heavy emphasis in his voice. Then he laughed and added 'You have the SRRC with you in any case, so you are safe!'

They were right of course. In my anxiety simply to get to this place I had forgotten about the regulations. It was easy enough to do that. After all, the radio was not my responsibility. But it mattered and I should have had it under control. Now I was just lucky Simon had for some reason decided not to use this opportunity to bring the whole excursion to a dismal end before it had even started.

Simon continued to stare at me and smile. There was no humour in the smile, only calculation. I squirmed inside but felt I had to stand my ground or lose whatever it was that I had come for.

Then I remembered the Thuraya in my pack. 'Not to worry,' I said, the relief causing me to smile. A childish sense of triumph nudged me into directing that smile directly back at Simon. 'I have the Thuraya, I'll use that. It's not the same as radio, but I'll call security directly on it and that will do instead. I'll ring them tonight and tomorrow morning again at the time of the radio check.'

'Good,' said Father Severino. He began waking fast towards the well. 'Then all is in order. Let's go!'

We followed him across the hot, stony open space between the clump of trees and the water point, where a group of women were gathered waiting their turn to fill the plastic buckets and jerry-cans they carried. I looked beyond them at the village where the huts seemed packed so close together that there wasn't a way in between them.

'This is not how they normally live,' said Father Severino. 'These people are refugees. They are packed together here in this place.'

'IDPs,' Simon corrected him with the school-boy pedantry that came, I knew, from the training courses that were given to him and his like, filling their minds with terminology and self-importance. 'They have not crossed any international border, so they cannot be classified as refugees.'

'They were driven here by the Toposa,' continued Father Severino, as though he had not heard the interruption or choose to ignore it. 'They lost everything they had. You can see they have no cattle. It was all taken from them. Now they have to depend on what we can give them and what they can grow. You see the maize field over there.'

'We should take a look at it afterwards,' I said. 'I would like to see what state their crop is in. We have been told that up in Boma the crop has been disastrous this year.' I looked across at Simon as I said this, challenging him to deny that he had provided this information and had in fact insisted on it.

'I do not know about how it is in Boma,' said Father Severino. 'But here it is growing still, almost ready for harvest and it is looking good, I think, although I am not an expert. The stalks are tall and the ears are fat. But it will not be enough to feed them all and it does not give them all the nutrition they need, especially not the children. Sister Lucy would like to start a proper clinic with supplementary feeding for the children, but it is too far for us to support and we do not have enough supplies. It needs someone else, really. I am hoping you may be able to…'

He broke off as a group of women caught sight of him and began to ululate in greeting. They came running over to the visitors, their wide open mouths showing large white teeth as they laughed.

This laughter that burst from their throats came out from somewhere deep inside, spontaneous, unfiltered, a straightforward expression of joy at meeting. It should have infected me, but instead I felt myself retreat inside. I found myself looking at them in the same old way - with the camera-lens eye of the outsider: the anthropologist, the traveler, the tourist.

They were tall and thin, like most Nilotic people, with fine, high cheekbones. Most of them wore a long blanket tightly draped over their right shoulder and wrapped loosely around their long, thin legs down to below the knees. The coppery red, earth-smeared skin of their arms was decorated with dozens of bracelets, bright plastic, metal, glass, and thick collars of beads adorned their necks. Their ears were pierced with great gaping holes in the lobes, the African way, with long, dangling earrings. An embroidered leather band circled their close-cropped heads. Others wore nothing more than a small piece of cloth around their waists and thick, multiple strands of beads around their calves, arms and necks. Their breasts were bare and innocent. That was the way it always seemed out here in rural Africa. The breasts of a woman were strangely asexual. However beautiful a woman might be, her breasts were always utterly and constantly linked to biological function, not to beauty or allure. Their size and shape drew your thinking always to number of children she must have borne and nursed.

That was true of this group, I observed. Some of the women carried babies wrapped in a cloth strapped round their backs. Once they had reached the priest, they stood still and some of them swung their babies round to the front so that they could nurse.

Within five minutes a group of fifty women had gathered around the priest, closing in on him, shouting and laughing with a warmth and an excitement that was far beyond what could ever have been induced by material expectation. They were shouting greetings I guessed. Father Severino smiled and replied to their cries intermittently, turning to the rest of us to explain, 'I don't speak their language, but I can say some words and also some in Murle and they understand.'

I looked at the sea of faces and to me it seemed at once that I was witnessing an act of open and frank adoration of the kind that came in books about latter-day saviours and prophets. It was not something I had ever liked the idea of. To my mind it had more to do with fanaticism than anything else. It was a look I thought I had seen in some of the faces in the religious art of the high Renaissance, the look on the faces of the shepherds and the Magi adoring the Infant Christ or of his disciples and family gazing up at him on the cross. And in those pictures the adoring contemporaries of the adored were always accompanied by some grandee patron from the artist's own times, anachronistically thrust into the narrative to satisfy the patron's sense of his own piety and value.

Of course that was my role here in this little tableau. The thought burst into my mind in a sudden bright gust of intellectual inspiration. For a moment I savoured it and took pride in my own cleverness. Then, almost at once, the taste turned sour in my mouth and the good feeling gave way to the habitual sense of shame that seemed to connect me directly to every rotten turn of thinking I had taken since my childhood. I looked around again and saw that the moment was past and I had missed being part of it forever.

Then I saw Father Severino being led by the arm and by the hand into the heart of this village that seemed more like a maze than anything else. I shook my head to clear it and joined my colleagues at the back of the throng.

The narrow passageway between the tightly spaced circular huts was dark and stuffy and I was immediately aware of a peculiar feeling of stepping backwards in time into an older Africa, untouched by anything brought to it from outside. There was a smell, too, not unpleasant – almost comforting, in a way, in its naturalness, the way the warm body of a mother must feel to her child. I thought about it, analyzing and disaggregating. I could clearly isolate the odours of damp earth and dried grains and the long stalks of drying grass in tight bundles being handed up onto roofs. Chickens ran flapping between my feet and in the small dark doorways tiny, pot-bellied children with spindly arms and legs, naked apart from a leather cord around their waists, stood in silent wonder watching the strangers pass like something from a fairy tale, possibly good, possible bad, strange and frightening.

I did not know if I felt or if I should feel happy to be here, deep in the heart of this other world that had every naïvely observable aspect of 'Africa' oozing from the pores of its deep red earth, or if I wanted to get out quickly, overwhelmed by the claustrophobia of the narrow, dark spaces between the huts and the staring eyes of naked children with distended bellies and dirty faces covered in earth and snot, across which the flies walked unhindered. If I was here to see things, then I could have seen it all better from the top of a tree or the roof of a vehicle.

If the people had still had their cattle there would have been more flies, of course.

I stayed at the back of the procession. I was thinking too much, which I knew to be a symptom of embarrassment, of not knowing my place in someone else's business. I did not want to pretend I was part of this or to fool myself into believing these people could see me in the same light in which they saw the priest.

At every house Father Severino paused to be greeted by the women who had emerged and now stood in front of their doorways with big, slow smiles and often tears and a flow of words in a language I would never know. I saw their long, slender arms reach out to clasp his hand, as though it could do something miraculous for them there and then through some quick gesture of blessing or something of the kind that would deliver manna from heaven.

'Mata!' After a while I was able to single out the word of greeting they spoke each time the priest came near. In return Father Severino would stop and clasp the hands that was reaching out to him and then gaze deep into the dark, tearful eyes, as though he had understood the flow of sound that was being thrown at him, whatever it was and whatever tale of suffering or uncertainty it had to tell, the voice of the world he had decided not to forget, even though it would have been so easy for the rest of the world to do just that.

I repeated the word back to them when it was my turn to be touched and held in the same smiling gaze despite my awkwardness at bathing in reflected glory. In the end I knew it was not surprising and I told myself it should not disturb me unduly, although I felt unable to respond in any meaningful sense beyond a mechanical acting out of what was expected. There was nothing natural in my being here and no reason for such warm and trusting intercourse. I could not pretend to be what others were – what one very particular other was – and it was driving me further down into my own reflecting mind and simultaneously out from the scene itself into cold, external observation of it. The women clung to

Father Severino and believed in him. The rest of the visitors were merely part of his retinue.

Yet I found that I did not mind this. I told myself that I had in fact expected nothing else, although the awareness of my own alienation from the things, and above all the people I purported to care about filled me with a sudden, overwhelming melancholy. I was a witness to a mutual love that was a million miles away from what I or my lot and their organizations could ever hope to achieve, not that any of them were in the slightest bit interested. To have the real bond that I was witnessing now and then to be able to help people in a true sense, it was necessary to know them and to love them. For a young Mexican priest that would mean living for most of the rest of his life out here, miles from anywhere, under-resourced and usually forgotten in this lost corner of the diocese of Torit. None of the rest of us was going to offer up that sacrifice.

At the same time it seemed to me that in some way I did envy the priest and that too seemed only natural. I envied the ease with which he conversed with the women, the way they wanted to talk with him and the way he listened back to them. When we reached the end of their tour, all the children lined up to shake the hands of the strangers and exchange the greeting word 'Mata!' which was the limit of our communication. They were nervous and at once bashful and bold, wanting to touch these unfamiliar, important beings who had entered their world like aliens appearing out of nowhere in low budget movie.

A single word and a smile before dashing back into the darkness of the huts.

Father Severino did not enter into any kind of analytical or speculative process at this point. He kept moving constantly, walking constantly, pausing briefly to listen and then walking on, oblivious to anything outside this engagement until he came to the end of where the human habitation had risen up out of the hard, rock-strewn earth. Here he turned briefly, still walking, to look back at the strangers he had brought with him into the world that he alone had found. 'Now we should meet the elders,' he said.

By now we had distanced ourselves a little from the houses and the women had left us. 'I have told the mothers that we will set up the clinic in a short while,' he said. 'Sister Lucy is going to sort that out now while we go over to where the elders are.'

'What about the boxes?' I asked. 'Can't we help?'

'That will be taken care of by Sister Lucy,' he replied, 'with the help of the women. They are very keen.' He led the way towards a group of trees where some figures could be seen sprawled out in the shade and seemingly motionless in the way that cows seem motionless when they sit low to chew the cud.

The distance to where the elders were gathered was about a hundred yards. The open space in between seemed to pack all the concentrated heat of the day into a force that was pushing against us as we walked across it, making our feet seem heavier to lift than they had been in the dark and shady places, while our faces were scorched and antagonized by the unhidden sun.

The old men lay silent and almost motionless, indolent with the indolence that comes with undisputed authority, large and powerfully built, surprisingly fat as well. Only when they were right up close and I felt able to raise my gaze against the glare did I notice that they were all naked, sharing a single large blanket spread in the shade under some trees. They did seem not interested in their visitors at all. They looked at us slowly without showing any emotion on their faces or uttering any sound, while Simon spoke in Murle and one of the young men who had come across to join us translated into the Jiye tongue. When Simon had finished there was a pause and then the old men replied, taking turns, and the young man translated into Murle from which Simon translated into English for the benefit of the rest of us. It seemed that they were talking about food and about cattle - the things they said they needed.

I suddenly became aware of thirst. Watching the old men as they reclined on the ground and listened without interest to the strangers made my mouth feel dry and old and the thirst made me irritable. I found it hard to fight against the prejudices that surfaced inside and urged my thoughts to swift conclusions. It was always that way when I had to deal with pastoralists. I saw the women working, farming or fetching water or firewood, like the Jiye women here, whose field of maize was now tall and ready for harvest, looking healthier that the crops I had seen in Boma; I saw the young men dance and fight and the old men take their ease; and I found it hard not to jump to the conclusion that once removed from the world of the cattle raid and long, lonely days tending the herds, the men would not adapt very easily to what came afterwards, when all that used to be was taken away. The women would continue to do the things that they had always done. They would work, they would bear children and they would survive. The men would turn into wasters and crooks.

We took our leave and walked back over towards the vehicle, where Sister Lucy had established herself under a large canvas sheet stretched from the roof rack at the back to the nearest tree branches strong enough to bear its weight, to which it was fastened. She had set out a fold-up table and two chairs together with a weighing scale. On the table there was a notebook, which she invited me to inspect. The names of mothers and their children with a series of statistics were set out in neat rows and columns.

A group of women with their muddy-faced, spindly, pot-bellied children and garlands of flies was sitting quietly in the shade nearby on a blanket that someone had spread for them.

'You should be helping,' I said, turning to Samuel. 'I thought you were nutritionist?'

Samuel smiled and looked over at Sister Lucy. 'We have already arranged that,' she said.
I turned away. They did not need any orders from me to sort themselves out.

Father Severino was waiting to take us on a brief walk to see the maize crop. There was more shade over here. Acacia trees lined the way to the planted field, spreading their mottled shade. I saw the maize stalks were as tall as Father Severino had told us, reaching high above our heads, like they would have done in the milpas back in his distant Mexico. I wondered if the crop comforted him with dreams of home. For myself, I do not like maize very much. It grows too tall. It blocks the view and hems you in. It is greedy too. I have read somewhere that it depletes the soil in a way the sorghum it has replaced across Africa never did.

The priest hardly seemed interested in the crop, as though he had only brought us over here because it was part of the programme. All the time as we stood and pretended we knew what we were seeing, fondling the fat, leaf-wrapped ears, he was telling us that his main concern was water and sanitation.

'The risk of disease is the biggest problem here,' he said. 'You can see how they are living and they have no facilities at all. They just go to the bush. There is a very high rate of gastro-intestinal infection among the small children. I think many may die.'

'It's always the same, Father' I said. 'They need water and sanitation, but we will probably give them food aid.'

I said this because it was the truth that I knew, but I also knew that it did not need saying.

'They will come to Boma for their food aid,' said Simon. 'There is no landing strip here and there will not be a food drop, eh, Daniel, not when their crop is as good as this?' He looked over at the Kenyan, who had spoken very little during the trip. I reckoned he had probably only come along in order not to remain alone and bored in Boma.

Daniel nodded, smiled briefly and then lit a cigarette without speaking. He offered the packet around and I joined Samuel in accepting one. As always I felt slightly nauseous when I reached the third or fourth drag, but I sucked the smoke in hard, nonetheless, as though it would help me to feel better or might even help me to reach the understanding I had expected.

In reality the whole thing seemed no different from anything else I had come across before. Except that Father Severino had shown an intimacy and care – call it love, almost – that I would never be able to feel, because I would never be given an opportunity to feel it, which meant that I would never be able to put my own humanity to the test in the way that he could. Not that it would have been a wise thing to do.

'We have given them a well!' said Simon. 'That is something very important.'

'You are right, Simon,' said Father Severino, smiling at him and patting him on the back in a gesture that if it had come from any other man would have been taken for condescension. 'It was an important thing to do and I think these people are very grateful. You can see they are using it. Without it in fact they could not survive here.'

'If we are camping we will dig a latrine this evening,' said John slowly. 'We will ask the men to help us dig it and then we will show them what it is and why it is important. If they can learn this, it will be the first step for hygiene.'

Father Severino smiled at him. 'You are also quite right, John,' he said. 'It will be a start and I am very grateful to you for it.'

We pitched the two tents a short distance from the Landcruiser and the temporary clinic. There was a small, modern one for Sister Lucy and a larger, WFP-style canvass one which would hold three of the men.

'Who sleeps where, then?' I asked. 'Should we toss a coin or draw straws?' I was being flippant, but my attempt at humour was sincere. I had a feeling that if I could make them laugh it might be a way back into their fellowship following the rupture I had brought about through my earlier outburst. In spite of everything, in spite of all the thoughts that had driven me out into the mental wilderness, I did not want to be alone. I wanted to restore things to the way they had been, to the comfortable tension of a slight, niggling antagonism that yet preserved a hierarchy and an order, placing me at the top with my half-way isolation justified as the loneliness of command. I could not make some sort of public apology and I could not just tell them I had been over-stressed. They would not have understood. They did not do things like that. My behaviour must just seem like yet one more example of my white-skinned, senior staff arrogance.

To them I must seem senior, of course. I came from Nairobi, where I spent most of my time in an office, while they slogged to and fro across this landscape, setting up their radios and tents, purifying their water and digging their latrines. They did the things you had to do out here without thinking, almost by instinct. Things I found difficult, because to me they were not the familiar activities of every day of my life. I was an outsider and a neophyte. I admired them, too, without being able to admit to it, for to do so would have been to further abase myself before them.

'You're the boss, sir,' said Samuel. 'Where do you prefer?'

'I don't mind, really I don't,' I said. 'What do you think?'

In the end we left the matter to be decided later on and went to help John with his pit latrine.

Simon had sent his translator to summon a group of young men to help and to learn. He seemed to have decided that the elders were beyond instruction in these matters. The young men stood now in a circle, listening. I noted that they were all powerfully built and were all tall. All of them were wearing tight shorts, some red, some yellow, of the thigh-hugging variety you might use for a work-out session in a gym back in Nairobi. Simon, John and Samuel were standing in the middle of the circle speaking slowly so that the translator could follow the words that issued – first in English from John in his deep base voice, then translated into Murle in Simon's higher-pitched whine – in order to translate them in his own quiet, almost whispered tone into Jiye. From time to time the men grunted, sometimes in unison, expressing their agreement at some point of particular wisdom or poignancy.

'We are teaching them why it is important for them to use the latrines,' said John, calling over to me. 'You see thus is all new for them. Out in the bush they can go anywhere they like and they move on. But now they must stay here and they are having problems with hygiene. They tell me many children have been sick, you see.'

After a few minutes the men began to dig with the tools they had brought. 'Come and see,' shouted John.

I walked across and stood and watched with the others as two young men dug down into the earth with heavy shovels. They were naked apart from the small leather loin-cloths they wore around their groins. In another time or place the sight of them would have had tourists' camera's clicking.

Samuel brought a bundle of thick tree branches over. 'We can use these to build the cover slab,' he said. 'This is not going to be a "VIP-latrine" Richards, just a straight-forward pit. We will not even line it, although that is the best.'

The men who were digging tossed spade-fulls of earth clear away from the edge of the pit with sharp, energetic thrusts. 'I have instructed them to throw the earth well clear,' said John. 'That way it does not just fall back in. If it is made properly and dug deep enough it can go on being used for several months. The problem is usually to convince people that it is a good thing to do. They do not like to use a hole in the ground like this. You know they think there may be evil spirits in the hole.'

He peered down into the hole, which was now a neat oblong several feet deep. 'That will do,' he said. 'We just need the slab and a cover for the hole.'

He turned back to address me, speaking slowly, didactically, as though I were one of the villagers learning this new skill from him: 'That is so that it does not stink and it keeps the flies away. Then we will build a shelter around the slab. For now we will just make a frame with the corner posts and put some blankets round it. Later they can make walls out of the earth, like the houses, with a thatched roof. They know how to do that. It is most important. People need to feel private and safe, you know. Especially the women.'

A woman came over with a bucket of water. 'This is for us to use for drinking,' said Simon.

Samuel and John looked into the bucket. 'It looks like it has too many impurities in it,' said Samuel, 'I'll get my bag.'

'Watch this, Richards,' he said when he had returned carrying his rucksack over one shoulder. He put it down on the ground and extracted a plastic bag from one of the side pockets. Out of it he took a fist-sized lump crystalline rock and held it up for Richard to inspect. 'Alum crystal,' he said. 'It will clear the water of the turbidity. It's a good thing to take to the field. I learnt that years ago.'

He dropped the small hard lump into the bucket and we watched as the water slowly cleared.

'Now we are ready for the night,' said John joining us. 'The pit latrine is built and the men have agreed to build one for every five households in the village.'

'Do you believe they will do it?' I asked.

'Maybe,' said John, slowly with same grave tone that had entered his voice when they had started to build the latrine. It was the tone of voice of a preacher, sure of his message and his mission, the same tone as when he prayed over food. 'I hope so. It is a pity we cannot stay to follow-up.'

We went back over to the vehicle, where Father Severino and Sister Lucy were dismantling the clinic, folding the furniture and storing the equipment in boxes.

'The load will be lighter going back tomorrow,' said Father Severino. 'We have distributed all the supplementary food we brought. The children are all malnourished but what can we do..?' He let the question hang for barely a split second before he answered it himself: 'We do what we can.'

Staring at him across the Landcruiser bonnet, it came to me, in a flashing, unexpected instant, that the fatigue brought on by the day's long drive through the heat and the immediate plunge into the vast and impossible task to which the young priest had committed himself would cast him down now, despite the refutation that was in these last softly spoken words. The sweat glistened on his forehead and beneath it there were lines that spoke of a weariness that was deeper than the mere effect of the day's labours. It was like seeing a sudden weakness where before there had only been strength, like a child seeing his father lose a fight.

Seeing this I kept my mouth shut. I wondered briefly if I should say something, ridiculous as it might seem coming from me, some words of encouragement. But I held back, not so much because of the disordered state of my own mind, but from a sudden awareness of something that did not have its origin within my own interior monologue, but was in some ways bigger than and indifferent to it, a sense of utter distance and isolation emanating from the priest, a private and lonely immersion in a world he had travelled far to discover, swimming deep and far out across his own vast sea.

And at the same time there was something else I could feel, an ugly little sense of triumph inside, the silent smirk that said *'I was right and there is no victory'*.

Father Severino wiped his brow with his sleeve and looked at him with the brief, reassuring smile that seemed to come to him so easily, as though snapping himself out of a hypnotic trance with a snap of his own fingers. 'Now we should think of our own meal,' he said. 'You must all be hungry as I am.'

He was right, of course. The lack of a midday meal never seemed to matter in the heat of the day, but as it cooled in the evening appetites always returned. That was a rule as sure as the rules that said the sun would set and the fires be lit.

The sky was orange now behind us in the west as the sun sprawled down onto its rocky bed, while over in the east it was a deep purple colour, almost black, and the first stars could just about be discerned, sparkling intermittently. There was not a cloud anywhere, which meant it would cool down nicely in the darkness.

'There will be food for us in the village,' said Sister Lucy.

'A feast,' said Simon. 'They have told me. They have no cows to kill, but they will kill a goat.'

'We will give them the vegetables we have brought and the salt,' said Sister Lucy. 'Please carry these boxes.'

We began to stroll towards the village. A new sound could be heard coming from the twilight beyond the well. I peered into the increasing gloom towards where I could see a group of young men in a circle dancing in the Nilotic fashion, taking turns in the middle to see who could jump the highest while the others sang and clapped their hands in a constant, strongly stressed iambic rhythm: clap-CLAP… clap-CLAP.. clap-CLAP. Around the fringes of this inner male group stood a wider circle of girls, egging the men on with shouts and laughter and occasional high-pitched shrieks of excitement. The men had no clothes on except their tight gymnastics shorts, their bodies otherwise unadorned. Their long thin limbs flexed with the dance and pushed against the hard earth in a slow, sustained and ancient rhythm, propelling them upwards over and over again high above the heads and shoulders of their clapping, chanting peers.

'Why do they want to dance now, just after they have lost so much?' I felt naïve in asking this question, but could not keep the words from spilling out into the space between us as we walked. I wanted to know the answer. I wanted to understand the way things were, so different from the way logic dictated, or my own sense of what was fitting or normal wanted.

'They have to dance,' said John. 'This is what the young men do all over the New Sudan in every tribe. The Dinka do the same. Have you never seen? They are happy, they are young and strong.'

'The girls are watching!' said Simon. 'Maybe their girlfriends. Or maybe they can catch a girlfriend of they look good or jump the highest.'

'Life continues,' said Father Severino in turn. 'The people can still celebrate life, even if they have lost so much. That is what is so wonderful about them!'

We reached the dancers and stood and watched for a while. There was nothing here but energy and sweat and the rhythmic clapping. It had no beginning or end, no shape other than the endlessly repeated upward thrusting into the night sky.

In the open space beyond the dancers, between the well and the houses, a fire had been lit. Strips of meat had been spread on a frame to roast and pots were boiling in the embers, balanced on stones. We sat down on the ground and Sister Lucy handed out plates. The women came and took the plates one by one, bringing them back piled with pieces of meat and bone. Then we ate in silence, chewing the tough meat, watched by the women. Behind us we could hear the dancers clapping and shouting. Above our heads the moon was shining.

When we had finished we stayed sitting on the ground, still silent, as though we all felt unsure of what to say here, strangers among a people we could not converse with. Then, in that sudden, disorienting, out-of-the-blue way that the things we were supposed to do but have forgotten all about come to us, I remembered the Thuraya in my pack. 'I'll go and call security,' I said and I raised myself stiffly on legs that were numb from sitting cross-legged for longer than my western ways were used to.

'That would be a good idea,' said John. 'It is already late now.'

I made my way back to the Landcruiser, opened the back and pulled out my pack. The torch was easy to find. I always left it at the top of everything else, so that I could have light quickly in the night without fumbling around for it in the darkness. I switched it on and directed the beam down into the rucksack as I rummaged with my other hand, expecting to find the heavy oblong block of the satphone easily enough. I felt everywhere twice over, but found nothing. In the usual way, still calm, I took everything out carefully, laying out the objects in methodical rows on the floor of the vehicle as I extracted them. But the Thuraya was not there and it was not in the side pockets, either.

A spasm of acute anxiety wrenched my stomach with a sudden nauseous cramp. The satphone was not there where it should have been. I knew it could not have fallen out, because the pockets had all been done up properly. The only logical conclusion had to be that I had left it behind.

It was Simon's fault, of course. I remembered now in the vivid flash-back mode of a racing, panic-stricken mind. I had been in the act of packing when Simon had come up with his stupid mocking questions and made me lose my concentration. I always had to be alone at that early morning time when I packed my things, but Simon had not respected that. He had intruded and I had lost my concentration.

That was the way I wanted to tell it to myself, but I knew it was not the true story, not the way it really was in my mind. The others had all brought something. They all had a role. They helped in the clinic and dug latrines. Even the well that was all that kept these people alive in this desolate spot had been given to them by Simon, of all people. And my job, my one lowly contribution based simply on the equipment that only I was permitted to carry, had been to look after the communications. And I had failed even in that. I was the one person who had brought nothing and had contributed nothing.

I wondered whether to tell them. I wondered about it for some time, waiting for them to come over from the fire and join me. But when I saw them coming at last I made up my mind to say nothing. It wouldn't make any difference and there was nothing I could do about it now. The day had been long and I was tired.

## 9.

*Later on Sunday night*
As they came closer, I made up my mind. A man's voice called out 'Hi, Richards, did you get through?'

I did not look up to see who it was and my mind was not sufficiently focused to distinguish the voice. It did not matter, anyway. I grunted in reply, deliberately smearing the sounds around my mouth on their way out so that my answer could have meant anything. Then I turned and hurried into the dark shadows of the scrubland, hunching my shoulder slightly as though holding the bulky handset to my ear.

I blundered across the rough terrain for about a hundred yards, away from the vehicle and away from the fire. Then I stopped. I could hear voices speaking in low tones. I was sure that one of them was Simon's. There was a woman, too, I could tell from the higher, smoother pitch. I froze and let myself melt into the tall dry grass at the edge of a maize field. I stayed like that for several minutes until the certainty that I had not been spotted had calmed my breathing. Then I began to be curious. The scene before me drew my attention out of myself and into it. I wanted to know who was with Simon and what they could be talking about out here in the darkness. I edged forward until I was close enough to hear what they were saying. The woman was speaking.

'We have brought it here,' she said. 'We have done what you said. They will take it across the border and they will bring your guns. We have kept the promise.'

'You have kept your promise,' said the man and I was sure now that it was Simon. There was a touch of menace in his voice. 'The priest has done nothing!'

'And he knows nothing!' hissed the woman. 'He must not know! That was our bargain and you must keep it.'

'Must?' I heard the sneer in the man's voice.

'If you do not, you know what I will do!'

'You accuse me of smuggling? What? Ah yes, the gold everyone is dreaming about. You will tell the commander that I have been abusing my authority. Isn't that what you told me? Young men from these refugees around here have been mining the gold that everyone says is here, our gold in our streams at the bottom of our mountains! That is your story. Young men that I control. My slaves, ha! ha!' The man laughed out loud now, a wild cackle like a frog call or a burst of small arms fire through the maize field that rustled with the evening breeze. Then he went on 'And you think he will believe this story of yours?'

'He will!' said the woman with the same vehemence in her voice. 'He will because it is the truth!'

'Where is the evidence? There is no truth without evidence. You know that…'

'Just do not tell Father Severino!' she said and now there was a different tone in her voice, softer, pleading. 'This is his life. This is what he is here for, his whole life and I must support him. He is a good man, a holy man. He is here to do God's work. One of the only ones…'

'And so you help us,' said the man, his bullying tone changing in turn to a softer, unpleasant drawl.

'The gold is here. That is enough,' said the woman. They will come here when you call on your radio, here where nobody knows and nobody sees a lorry in the dark. They will take it and bring your guns.'

'Do not talk like this!' said the man. 'You have no idea. You only guess.'

'I know you have ambition.'

'Whatever you think you may know, you can keep it to yourself!'

The voices fell silent. I strained to see through the gloom, but could make nothing out. Then I heard footsteps. Just one person. Before I could move Sister Lucy appeared no more than five yards from me walking fast and sure-footedly through the darkness.
She must have seen me, but she gave no sign of it. She just carried on past me towards the vehicle, beyond which the flickering light of the fire could be seen.

I waited for the man to follow, but he did not. I carried on waiting, afraid to expose myself.

Then I heard voices again. Simon's and that of another man, who spoke very softly so that I could not make out his words or even the tone of his voice. Their exchange was short and then lapsed into the silence of the bush, just the wind in the acacia tree branches and the insects.

I kept still until I was sure no-one would come and then made my own way back to the Landcruiser. I went to the back and pulled the light-weight sleeping bag out of my pack. I had bought it in Nairobi a couple of weeks before especially for this trip. I enjoyed going around camping and outdoor shops. They fed a feeling that I was already embarked on adventure, as though the equipment alone could take me into the mystery of the vast, lonely landscapes where I would survive with its help.

A sudden image came into my mind. The American who had walked into my office in Nairobi to tell me about the persecution and suffering of the Christian, pig-rearing Mabaan tribe on the fringes of Blue Nile province, a tall man carrying a huge backpack onto which every conceivable expedition gadget was attached by karabiners, like glistening glass balls dangling from the branches of the Christmas trees of dimly remembered childhood. I told myself to despise the stranger. He worked for one of those weird evangelical outfits, full of Bible tracts and naïve ideas about development and aid. But it had not been the truth. I never told the truth to myself. The man had spent weeks on end walking to places where the rule book would not let me step out of a light aircraft for a couple of minutes and the truth was that I envied him. My dreams were always there walking into the bush, into the vast emptiness, alone and self-sufficient.

I turned to see John standing nearby with a mug of tea in his hand. I did not want to get into a conversation with him. 'I'll sleep in the tent,' I said, 'Or maybe even out here under the stars.' Above our heads the night sky was a spangled tent of stars. If I could just spend some time looking upwards at them I would clear my head of all the mess that was swirling in it.

'The ants will eat you, or else a hyena,' laughed John. 'Better in the tent.'

He and the others set about preparing their own sleeping gear. Daniel offered round the cigarettes and I took one, leaning against the radiator of the Landcruiser and gazing up at Orion with his dogs.

In the old times I used to take pride in pointing the stars and the constellations out to them, at first just to my wife, but later there had been the child, too. Orion was always the easiest because the three stars of the belt. You followed it one way and you came to Sirius, the brightest star in the sky, and the other way, more or less the same distance, took you to Aldebaran, which I used to tell them was the eye of the Bull, 'red and baleful.'

'Red and baleful' the child repeated. 'Red and baleful,' wondering what baleful meant but not wanting to ask in case knowing it spoilt the magic.

Father Severino came around from the back of the vehicle and took up a place next to me, also leaning back against the vehicle and looking up at the sky. 'They are beautiful,' he said. 'Sometimes at the end of a long day – usually a very frustrating day – I go outside and I look up at the stars. It's better up on the plateau, you know, where we have the school. There you see them so close you can almost touch them.'

He paused. I finished my cigarette and threw it down onto the hard, stony ground, reaching out with my foot to rub out the glowing butt, even though I knew there was no risk of it setting fire to anything.

I did not want the priest to be here with me. There were no words in my mind. There had been before we came here, based on the expectation of what we should find. Now that mirage had melted and I could find nothing inside myself apart from a growing sense of embarrassment at the gulf that I could feel opening up, not just between the two of us, but between myself and everyone else in the whole group, all of them, the people in the village, the whole of South Sudan, humanity. My mind was full of the things I had heard just a few minutes before. It did not shock or excite me. That was the stupid part of it. It was almost as though I could have expected to hear what I had done, or if not that then something similar, some other story about the way things were out here or might be, a mixture of truth and imaginings that had no consequence since nobody was ever going to see it or care about it.

'You are thinking?' Father Severino's words interrupted my thoughts with a questioning tone that was irritating and pedantic in its simplicity. To my relief he answered himself before I could think of anything to say. 'It has been a long day and most of it was on the road, I know. Somehow it is always like that here. The roads are so bad and places are always so far apart that when you get there where you are going it is already time to pack up and leave.'

The rules of conversation required some sort of response from me at this point, just to show that I was listening and agreed, or at least did not strongly disagree, with what the priest was saying. I mumbled 'Yes,' and then added that I was tired. I loathed the thought that Father Severino might choose this moment to ask me if I had found what I had been looking for, the magical healing balm that he had promised. I did not think that I could lie about that. 'I'm glad we came,' I said.

'You saw the people?' There was a kind of urgency in his voice, as though the words were burning the inside of his mouth before he let them out. 'They need help. They are alone here and they have nothing. No-one even speaks their language. Most people have never heard of them. We are all they have and we do so little. You saw the children?'

'Yes, they look malnourished. Of course they've all got worms.'

'Yet they are so trusting, their need is so innocent,' Father Severino continued, speaking quickly with a fervour that put my nerves on edge. Here in the misery and helplessness of this small, forgotten community the priest had found the need he could respond to, the answer to the question he had borne, the beloved for his love. But for me there was just dirt and sweat.

'You find it a lot in South Sudan,' I said. I expected to be challenged, to be told that this small group was different, because of their location, because of their vulnerability, because no-one knew about them or cared.

Bu the priest only nodded. 'I have not traveled to other areas,' he said. 'I suppose you have seen a lot of misery and suffering.'

'I don't know, Father,' I said, finding relief in the distance that came this way of addressing him. 'I seem to have spent most of my time sitting in planes.'

A torch flickered as the flap of the temporary shelter around the long-drop opened and John emerged. 'It is working fine,' he called to them, as he approached. 'A good day's work!'

'Yes,' said Father Severino, straightening himself up and reaching forward to clasp his hand in greeting. 'You have done such good work today. But do you think they will use it?'

'You will have to reinforce the message,' said John. When he spoke as an expert, a solid self-confidence seemed to enlarge his physical presence, filling his tall frame outwards and putting flesh on the bone. His voice was deep and rich, the voice of a leader, self-assured within his own land and among his people. 'I have told them they must dig more so that everyone is using. But it will take more than that. They will not be convinced at first. There must be meetings. The elders should be consulted. Then a committee has to be formed for hygiene and sanitation. Usually that is the job of the women.'

'Always the women!' said Simon, joining them out of the darkness. 'Really it is the women who manage everything. They will be the leaders of the New Sudan!' He laughed, as he always did, so that it was impossible to gauge whether he meant this remark as a serious comment or a joke.

The querulous voice inside my head wanted to question Simon on this point. In my mind the exchange started 'Are you being facetious?' and then immediately broke down as Simon asked what facetious meant and the explanation became long and complicated and in the end took the whole point away. Instead I grunted slightly and Simon looked across in a way that suggested that he had understood the meaning I intended.

'When I come here, I feel so much love,' said Father Severino. 'It makes me humble inside. In reality I know these poor people give me more that I could ever give them.' In the darkness the white of his teeth could be seen as he smiled.

Daniel and Samuel joined us, followed by Sister Lucy, who said a brief good night and then retired to her tent. Daniel handed the cigarette packet round.

'I'll buy you a pack in Loki,' I told him as I took one. 'I'm sorry to be always on the scrounge.'

Daniel smiled briefly and said nothing in reply, as though making it clear that the damage I had done would not easily be healed. It troubled me. It had done so from the very moment I had let the shout leave my mouth in an outburst of fury at the sound of his radio desecrating the silence of the dark outside the claustrophobic nightmare of my tent in a way that did not bring the solace of company but simply ripped up the ordered flow of thoughts in my head. I had just wanted to switch off the hideous lonely sound of the preacher's Deep-South Southern Baptist drawl that was eating into the alien night.

I lit the cigarette and waited to see which way the conversation might swing. Samuel and John were making a fire from small twigs so that they could brew up water for tea. When there was a big enough heap in the middle of the small circle of stones with which they had shaped the hearth they lit it and stood the battered aluminum kettle, which I recognized from the SRRC compound, on a platform of three larger stones in the middle. The dry maize leaves and bits of paper they were using for kindling flared up quickly and the men sat down around it to watch the fire catch and the water slowly come to the boil. I guessed this was the best use the paper could have been put to.

'How do you feel camping out here, Richards?' asked Simon. It was one of those little questions he asked as though he sought under a cloak of innocence to extract as much irritation as he could from the slight mocking pinprick. His words and his voice seemed to be always on the verge of condescending, tinged with the slight suggestion that I was the least experienced, the least competent, that I alone might find the toughness of the experience beyond my capacity to endure, out here in the wild true heart of Africa, so very far beyond the soft beds and electronic comforts of my safe, distant world. The words always seemed chosen to suggest that I did not belong here.

Tonight I did not care. I did not know what I had seen, but it had changed things. I just felt tired, really tired at the end of a long day and the cigarette was making me feel nauseous.

'I think we are quite safe,' continued Simon. 'Safe enough from Dr. Melchior, ha ha!' He laughed, as if talking about the feared and loathed pro-government faction-leader were some kind of joke.

'What about the Toposa?' I asked. 'What is to stop them from coming back?'

I looked across at Father Severino. He said nothing.

'That will not happen,' said Simon. 'Do not worry! The Toposa have taken the cattle. There is nothing else they want. They are far away now. They will not come.'

'If there was any chance of that the people would be different,' said Samuel. 'Isn't that right?' He turned to Simon seeking his agreement.

'Yes,' said Simon. 'They would be fearful, if they thought the Toposa were nearby. They would already have come to Boma to escape!'

'It is a blessing if they are left in peace to rebuild their lives after the massacre,' said Father Severino. 'But security will be a problem here. You know that, Simon. And it is your responsibility.'

'I have told them they can come to Boma,' said Simon, suddenly serious, sensing a challenge to his authority and competence and reacting at once. 'They will come to Boma. I have told them.'

'What about their maize crop?' I asked. I had to challenge him now, whatever he said. It was all a lie and I wanted him to feel something from my words other than stupid, dumb acceptance of the story he was telling.

'They will come when it is harvested within two weeks. I spoke with the elders.'

I had realized at the time that not all of Simon's conversation with the elders was being translated, but it had not occurred to me that they might be talking about moving the community up the road to Boma without telling the rest of us. But then Simon was part of the administration, part of the crude, rigidly authoritarian police state that controlled everything including which personnel from which humanitarian organizations might enter and where they could go. It had nothing to do with me. If anything, my job was to keep on the right side of people like Simon. I might have been bothered once. There were humanitarian implications... But I did not care now. Not even after what I had heard this evening, whatever it meant. Nothing had been very clear anyway.

'What about massacres, though?' asked Father Severino. 'There have been so many.'

'You are talking about the Toposa?' asked John.

'No,' said Father Severino. 'I was thinking about Dr. Melchior, since Simon mentioned him just now. You said earlier that he had been responsible...'

'Ah yes,' said John. 'That was long ago. More than ten years. That time we were winning the war, like now. He thought he was not going to get his share of the power so he changed sides.'

'That was down in Bor, yes?'

'It was. The Nuer militias slaughtered hundreds of innocent women and children and all of Bor County was left empty. The Dinkas from Bor County who survived all ended up in the camps in Labone and places down there near Uganda.'

'I know, I have been there,' I said.

The plane had circled three times before it landed on the dusty yellow strip that ran down the middle of a lush green field, surrounded by mountains that were clad in a jungle of mixed woodland and bamboo. This was a security precaution. The mountains belonged to the LRA. They might fire at the plane or attack the airstrip. Their loyalties were to no-one other than themselves, but they were armed by the Government of Sudan.

The plane landed without incident and we were met by people from the NGO that ran the camps and taken quickly away in four-wheel drives that bounced at high speed along the dirt track.

Hidden from sight by the stands of bamboo, forty thousand Dinkas were living in three straggling villages along a valley full of tukkuls, all of them clustered among the maize fields, none of them very far distant from the camps. The threat from evil in the forested hills kept them huddled in their valley.

I had slept well that night in the mountain cool, despite the rustling of rodents in the roof above my head, to be woken at dawn by a large cockroach climbing up the inside of my mosquito net and falling onto my chest.

The next day had been spent fretting about the value of humanitarian assistance in a 'complex' emergency like this one. I had seen children everywhere, a localized demographic supernova in response to the relative security and the certainty of the food deliveries that were needed to supplement the maize the villagers grew. Food aid created dependency, I had concluded, and did not slow exponential population growth. And that in turn fed the cycle of poverty and malnourishment. There was no solution in that, just an endless postponement and the prospect of endless dependency.

The people were living in a world without cows, a changed world for them farming maize and lining up for the food aid distributions. When the peace came the SPLM was planning to move them back to where they had come from down in the empty toic. I had wondered if the people would be able to go back to a lifestyle left behind a generation before, or if they would drift into the shanty towns of the proposed New Sudan. Perhaps they would simply stay in the camps.

'It was a genocide,' said Samuel. 'They killed everyone they could. They gunned them down and burnt the houses. My family were killed in that massacre.'

We sat in silence for a minute. Then I felt compelled to ask 'Do you think he will do it again?'

'Not now,' Simon said. 'He does not have the same forces. He came back from the North with nothing.'

'Can the Dinka live with the Nuer, though?'

'Can the Toposa live with the Jiye or with the Turkana?' asked John. 'I think we can all live together if there is justice and development. That is what we need.'

'First there must be peace,' said Samuel.

'Peace is coming,' said Simon. 'We shall have everything in the New Sudan.'

'But for now let us drink tea,' said John, squatting down and reaching forward to lift the boiling kettle off the fire.

Tea was something good. Sometimes it was a whole lot better when they made it the Kenyan way with powdery loose-leaf tea dust, water, milk and sugar all brewed up in the kettle. It came out sweet, but strong too, so that it gave your brain the kick it needed to wake it out of the sleep-charm the heat was putting on it. All John had done this time was to boil up the big old kettle full of water and put some tea bags and sugar in the mugs they had brought with them. He poured the hot water into the mugs now and we each took one. The real thing about tea, though, was that you drank it together, usually after you had done something, like work a hot and frustrating day or walk a great distance through the heat. It was always in some way a reward you shared like a team.

'Just how I like it,' I said, 'hot and wet.'

Nobody responded or laughed. Whatever humour this trivial, worn out phrase might carry was bound up in a context that had nothing to do with this place or these men and there was no interface, as though I had deliberately, even perversely sought to communicate in a way that was bound to fail. There was not much more to be said, anyway. We were all tired. We drank in silence, staring at the embers of the fire or out into the dark landscape or up at the stars, low hanging and bright against the moonless black of the sky. When we had drained our mugs we took turns to use the shower John and Samuel had rigged with plastic water bag suspended over a branch and then went to sleep, the four Sudanese crammed into the tent and Daniel in the back of the Toyota, on the seat where he had slept throughout the journey down. Only Father Severino remained with me, the two of us still leaning back against the radiator grill at the front of the vehicle so that our gaze, when looking straight ahead was upwards into the heavens.

For a while neither of us spoke. I did not feel any desire to continue the dialogue we had left unfinished. A sense of shame, greater than any disappointment could have been, made me awkward with the priest. There was something I was supposed to have seen, but had not, something I was supposed to find, but which had remained unfound, and something I was not supposed to see but had seen and this had set a gulf between us that I could not bridge without an awkwardness which I did not want to face up to now.

Eventually it was Father Severino's words that cut the taught wire of silence that stretched between us. 'It seems only we two are still awake,' he said.

'Sometimes, Father, I fall asleep so quickly I don't even take my clothes off. I just drop onto the bed and I am gone,' I said in reply, feeling the tension sag and letting the trivial, inconsequential words that kept us safe from facing the harder things gush out in a fountain. 'Those are the good times when I really sleep well. Other times it does not matter how tired I am or how hard I've worked, I just can't stop my mind from working. I sit and look at the stars and I simply don't feel tired. Sometimes ideas come and I want to write them down, but then they seem to melt away before I can sort them out coherently.'

'I know what you mean,' said Father Severino. 'I used to think I was going to be a writer. I would write novels and stories about my village and the people who lived there, ordinary people. They live their lives in a place and it defines them. Their fathers lived there before them and the same Huicholes came down from the mountains with their big baskets on their backs – the ones we call cacaixtles - on their way down to the desert for the peyote and the people still the same stories about them as they always did and still look after the children they sometimes leave behind. I thought I would write about one of those children.'

He turned as he said this so that instead of staring up at the stars he was now looking directly at me as he spoke, serious, but calm, like a consultant at his patient's bedside. Then he added 'Do you want to know why I wanted to write about the children?'

I had not expected the conversation to take this turn. I felt vaguely unsettled, but at the same time aware that the questions I had dreaded about my inner response to what I had seen that day were not about to appear. 'Yes, tell me,' I said.

'I saw myself as the little child who is left there by the Indians as they go through the village on their way to the desert.' Father Severino smiled as he said this, not with self-mockery, but as if he were remembering a feeling from the distant past that was still precious to him. 'I sometimes tell myself that is why I am so passionate about these people – because they are a small, outcast group all alone in the desert, like the Huicholes I remember from my childhood.'

He smiled again and let his gaze drift back upwards to the stars. 'They used to say it was true. My skin was darker than the others and they used to say I had been adopted, what we call a *'recogido'.'*

I said nothing. My eye was caught by the sudden flash of a shooting star that floated briefly across the sky and disappeared suddenly into the blackness.

'So I feel these are my people,' continued Father Severino. 'It is as though I have adopted them. I feel close to them, closer than with any of the others, and I find everything I need in this warmth I share with them, as though they were my family.'

He lapsed into silence for a moment and then asked, 'What about you, Richards? Forgive me, these two days I have asked you so many questions. Perhaps you take offence? But tell me. Tell me there is someone or some people for you, like this.'

'I know what you are getting at, Father,' I said. A sudden rush of tenderness, like a burst of unexpected enthusiasm, welled up inside me towards this man that I had only just come to know. At first he had just been admirable in his self-sufficiency and the practical nature of what he gave in apparent love, real selfless love, to the people he had come to spend his life with. But it was more, I knew, something gentle as well as tough shining through in all that he did, that drew me to the priest. The instinct had told me at the moment of our first meeting, as though it were my brother, long-lost but found again, recognized by an immediate instinct that defied definition. And now, knowing the darkness that was around him in all his naïve, straight-forward goodness made me feel almost protective, as though he were my younger brother. 'I wish I could feel the same,' I said.

For a moment I might have really meant these words, spoken now out of desire to be kind and not to disappoint. Yet at the same time my solitude bore down on me in the complacency with which I contemplated my failure. In my own eyes, I was also aware, it gave me a heroic stature, which I looked on at the same time with self-mockery and scorn. I was a lonely figure destined to die alone somewhere in the toic, where nobody would know and nobody would care.

The dialogue stayed inside my mind. Nothing ruptured the good feeling that there was between us. I liked that, liked standing here with the priest and looking up into the sky without saying anything more, watching to see if another shooting star would pass.

After a time Father Severino yawned. 'I think now I am a little tired,' he said. 'The day has caught up with me.'

'OK, you go ahead Father. I'll shower after you.'

The priest yawned again and smiled. 'You are a good man, Richards,' he said. 'I could feel it when we met the first time. You have a good soul that has beauty. You see things and you care, you do not just pass by on the other side.

'But, you know, I feel you keep some distance. Perhaps you have been damaged in a way that I do not know and I cannot help…No,' he said, after a moment's hesitation, 'that is not what I mean. It is more as if you have wandered somewhere and got lost, fallen down where nobody can find you anymore…'

'Anyway,' he added, straightening himself up. 'Maybe we have talked enough for today. It is time to sleep. I'll say goodnight.'

He went round to the side of the Landcruiser and opened one of the doors to take out his pack and get a towel for the shower.

I reverted to gazing up at the stars, waiting for my turn.

When Father Severino came back from the shower, I called out to him 'Tell me, Father, did you understand everything Simon said when we were with the elders?'

'Yes, why?' The priest seemed puzzled.

'I just wondered. How did they react when Simon told them they would have to move up to Boma? Did they like that? Do they want to go? Do they have any choice? And if they don't, where does that leave you?'

'Are you angry, Richards?'

'No, I'm not angry. But then I don't know if I should be. I didn't understand what was going on back there.'

'Well, they will have to move.'

'And you are happy with that?'

'Maybe it will be better.'

'They don't get to choose, though, do they?'

'No, they don't.'

'So why don't you give me a straight answer when I ask you if they want to move?' I felt the old stubbornness inside rising up to challenge the whole world. In the end everyone had an agenda to do with themselves. You couldn't push Simon and his lot too far without finding yourself thrown out, so you had to compromise, even if you were an idealistic priest from some Latin American barrio, it didn't make any difference in the end. What mattered was your life, so if you had chosen this place, these people to fill your life and give it meaning, then you would end up having to compromise. It was always like that. Everyone ended up doing it.

'Good night, Father,' I said before Father Severino could reply. Then I crossed the empty space to the shower. When I came back out, wondering whether the priest might be waiting for me with some lame self-justification, I found myself alone.

# 10.

*Monday Morning*
I was in the same placed, leaning back against the Landcruiser bonnet, when dawn brought the first streaks of light across the eastern sky and the stars began to fade one by one from view until only Venus was left, brighter than the others in the dark west. I had felt no desire to sleep and the thought of disturbing the others inside the vehicle, or rather of having to interact with them, had made me hesitate at first and finally back away from opening the door in order to get in and lie down. So I had just stayed leaning, uncomfortable and eventually cold, letting his thoughts drift and watching the constellations drift slowly over my head.

When there was enough light to see my way around clearly, I eased myself forward, stiff and awkward, and stumbled over to the new latrine to relieve myself. I did not feel sleepy, but the lack of sleep was affecting me, making my movements heavy and difficult to coordinate. I felt irritated, desperate for the bitter, foul-tasting stimulus of instant-coffee. The sounds that always filled these early morning vigils were coming from the tents – grunts and awkward snorts, a short, staccato burst of snoring and then a long sigh. The thin canvas walls gave them a loud, indelicate intimacy that fed my habitual impatience.

At least in this place there was no point in waiting for the others to rise or for the village women to come and take charge. There was nothing to prevent me from acting for myself. I picked up the kettle and shook it to check that there was still water in it. Then I set myself to gathering a small bundle of dry twigs from the ground under the acacia trees and built up a small new fire in the warm, still smouldering ashes. I pulled a box of matches and a roll a toilet paper out of my pack, ripping long strands of paper from the roll to scrumple up and stuff under the pile of twigs as a firelighter.

The challenge was always to get the fire going with a single match. This time it was easy and, once the twigs had caught, I slowly heaped on some of the smaller logs that were half burnt and hot from the night before. Then I placed the kettle on top of the large stones set on either side of the fire and sat down on the ground to wait.

The day started in the usual messy way. Each person got up when the growing heat got to him and some had more endurance or more inertia than others. Sister Lucy was the last to join the group at the fire, adding her mug to the others as we all waited for the kettle, now filled to the top, to boil again. The background sounds of loud, active life coming from the village switched suddenly into sharp focus as a laughing, singing group of women made their way to the well. Nobody said much beyond exchanging greetings until the water was poured and the first sips of coffee burned their lips and magically released their minds.

Daniel lit a cigarette and held out the packet the way he always did, mechanically, not so much inviting the fellowship of shared indulgence as obeying established convention. As always, I took one. It was early, of course, but I wanted the drug, just as I wanted the coffee, anything my mind could categorise as a stimulant that might pull the scattered fragments of my being together, pick me up and shove me into the world to face the day.

Father Severino had sat down next to me. 'So how did you sleep?' he asked. 'You look tired.'

'I'm fine,' I said, aware that to tell this obvious lie was like holding a door closed and equally aware that I lacked some sort of inner impulse that would have permitted me to open it, now or at any other subsequent more opportune time. 'Did not feel like sleeping last night. It just did not come.'

'Did you lie down at all? I did not hear you get in the truck.'

'No, in fact I stayed out. I was watching the stars.'

'So you did not sleep at all?'

'No.'

'I hope you will be ok today.'

'Don't worry, Father. This will keep me going.' I held up my coffee mug. 'This is my third cup of coffee. I'll probably sleep a bit on the road on the way back this afternoon. What is the programme today, anyway?'

'We have to complete the clinic,' said Father Severino, looking across at Sister Lucy, who nodded in reply. 'And maybe you have work to do for your survey.'

'Of course, Father,' I said. 'I was forgetting. Must be the lack of sleep. We have to do the survey. I need to include this community in our report for what it's worth, don't I?' I was not able to prevent the tone of my voice from conveying the way I felt about this empty exercise and I did not have the energy or the spirit to even try. 'And I guess we can get all the nutrition data we need from Sister Lucy?'

Sister Lucy nodded again.

Simon looked at the large, complex face of his wristwatch. 'Time for the radio check,' he said. 'Are you going to do it on the Thuraya?'

I felt a special tension inside me, like an actor about to step out and make his big speech. I had been expecting this moment without trying to work out how I would get beyond it. I had just known it would come, like a ditch that had to be jumped. I considered whether to maintain the pretence. Some words formed themselves, a justification for going off into the bush to make the call alone and undisturbed, but even as this pathway was opening up, another part of my thinking self was convinced that it would not do. I could not conceal the absence of the bulky handset, twice as big as even the most old-fashioned mobile phone, from my hand. And I was tired, in any case, too tired for a moment or two to bother with anything anymore.

'I haven't got it,' I said.

'What do you mean? Haven't got what?' asked Samuel. He suddenly looked uneasy.

'I mean I didn't bring the Thuraya. I forgot it, left it behind at the compound.'

'But last night?'…

'I did not make a call. I just said I did to keep you lot quiet.'

I said this softly. The words came out flat and dull and when I had finished nobody said anything else. I looked around and imagined I could see the vestiges of whatever respect the others might have had for me and their willingness to follow me on this mission evaporating in the knowing looks they exchanged across the fire.

'Well, we'll be back this evening,' I said. 'I'll explain it to them then.'

I stood up and took my mug over to the plastic container where they kept the kitchen things and then packed my rucksack and put it into the back of the Landcruiser. Then I joined in with the others packing the tents and other equipment. We worked in a silence which to me seemed heavy with unspoken reproach. When we had finished Samuel went to join Sister Lucy and Father Severino at the clinic, leaving the rest of us to await the arrival of Simon's group of interpreters to go with us for the survey work.

The silence remained unbroken, hanging like a drawn weapon between us, driving me away. In the end I had to find a reason to get away. 'I'll go and see the clinic while we wait,' I said, clutching at the first reasonable seeming idea. 'Maybe I can get the data from there.'

I handed the pile of forms to John and walked away without waiting for a reply.

There was already a small crowd of women with their pot-bellied, emaciated children sitting on the blanket under the trees. Sister Lucy had set up her fold-away table and weighing scales and was examining a child in the arms of its mother, while Samuel measured its arm circumference with a cardboard strip. I went over to stand behind Samuel, looking over his shoulder at the naked child. Its face was dusty and there was caked-on snot under its small, scarcely formed nose. Flies flitted around its eyes, occasionally landing and walking briefly with jerky, irritating movements across the checks and eyebrows. I found myself wanting the woman to do something about them, to flick them away or cover the face with a protecting cloth, but she stood, as though unaware and followed the movements of Sister Lucy's hands as she probed into the tiny mouth propped open briefly with a wooden spatula. When she took the child from its mother to weigh it on the scales, it cried out in a loud, piercing baby's wail that continued until it was safely back where it wanted to be in its mother's arms.

I wanted to feel something, an upwelling of compassion, or shame or guilt, any of the deep, violent emotions that had driven me in the past in other places where the poor and the hungry stood in lines with their babies and children waiting to be saved, but I found nothing, not even a clinical, detached interest or the purely intellectual consciousness that I was engaged in something fine and good; I found nothing, not even a real sense of relief when the baby's distressed howling subsided.

And, as always, I felt again the need to break the silence that was driving me into the outer darkness where all I ever found was the sterile closed circuit of interior monologue. 'Samuel,' I said. 'I did not want to disturb you and Sister Lucy, but I was just wondering about the data for the survey. Are you going to get it?'

'Don't worry,' said Samuel. He smiled briefly. I had come to consider him the most easy-going of my companions and it seemed to me that there was a hint of sympathy in the look that Samuel gave me now. 'I'm writing the measurements down for each child here, so we will have some figures for infant malnutrition.'

'Thanks,' I said. 'Can I do anything or shall I go with the others?'

An unfamiliar worried look came into Samuel's eyes for a moment. He wrinkled his brow and looked down, avoiding eye-contact, as though he were ashamed. I had never asked to be told what to do. I always knew. I was the one who always said we should do this or do that, but now here I was acting as though I had lost the sense of where I was going and where the others should follow.

The moment of silence that hung between us was making us both feel awkward. I broke it with a cough too forced and false to have fooled anyone. 'Sorry! I know, I'll go with the others as usual. We can get round a lot of houses I'm sure. Just came over to check on you. I'll go back now.'

I said goodbye to Sister Lucy and went back to the Landcruiser.

When I got there, I found the others had left already. I looked over towards the village. A group of women were gathered around the well, taking turns to pump water into the clay pots and plastic containers they had brought with them to fill. They were always there, I thought, not the same ones, of course, but always a group of women.

The well was their life, a place to meet each other, to talk and gossip. People always looked for a point around which to come together, the fire at night, a well like this one, a home.

Once upon a time I had had a home. It seemed so long ago that I could not remember how it had felt to live within that safe, sure world, where company was familiar and guaranteed, a warmth that came from unforced contact, answering visceral needs. The places I stayed now were just lonely rooms with a bed, a flat, dead extension of the emptiness I felt at all times, the inside reflected on the outside in an endless hell from where was no release.

What if I were to die? I had sometimes called out melodramatically, especially in the early days when the accident still left fresh, surprisingly physical memories across my dreams and waking thoughts, to the God I did not believe in and did not trust, to kill me, to take me away from an environment that brought nothing but pain and the promise of more pain, but now I wondered with an immediate horror that came from confronting an abyss infinitely more vast than anything I had ever imagined before, what it would it be like if death was not a switch to shut this off forever, but the beginning of an eternal perpetuation of the same horror, a vacuum of infinite solitude from which there could be no escape.

I set off towards the well, looking up briefly to greet the women but at the same time quickening my pace in order to get past them, frightened that they might detain me with kindly meant calls and gestures, obliging me to interact in whatever way I could through signs and smiles, to establish the very contact I craved but shunned with so much inner dread.

The village itself was quiet; the dense compactness had a forbidding air, like the outer wall of a fortress that I must penetrate. I tried to remember the route we had followed the day before with Father Severino, wondering at the same time where the priest was now. I should have asked Sister Lucy and then sought him out first to be my guide. The huts crowded close in around me. I turned a corner and was lost almost at once inside the maze of narrow paths between them.

For several minutes I blundered on, quickening my pace without meaning to and looking up as briefly as I could as I passed at the men and women who stood in doorways and the small, dusty children who flitted through the shadows. They were watching me. There was no hostility in the way they were looked at me, but I felt a strong compulsion to avoid eye contact. I wanted just to find my colleagues and hide myself at the back of the group, a nondescript participant in the exercise they were carrying out.

At one point I thought I could make out Simon's sharp voice behind one of the houses, but the house was packed up close against its neighbour so that I could not see any way past it in order to work out where the sound was coming from. I felt my heartbeat accelerating and I knew this was the onset of panic. I had experiences it from time to time throughout my life – as a child lost on a country walk and later as an adult at times that seemed so trivial that to remember them always brought on an unbearable self-loathing and shame. It had happened often enough when I had been stuck in endless unmoving traffic jams on the unfamiliar streets of some big third-world city, unsure of where I was, which direction I should take and yet unable to move. The feeling always came in a sudden claustrophobic rush. My temples throbbed and at the same time there was an unbearable tightness in my chest and a pounding that was in neither place but somehow, abstracted from it, as though forming part of my mind's awareness of the experience rather than the moment itself, shutting out all rational thought in a blinding urge to run fast away from where I was, to anywhere all, but away from where I was.

When the feeling came you had to reassert your rational self to regain the hold you needed to have on what was what and formulate some sort of procedure to get from the here and the when of the moment you could not cope with to the safe place your mind had fabricated. You did this at first by not allowing your pace to quicken. You turned round and retraced your steps through the maze. You smiled at every child every woman and every man who looked down at you from the conical rooftops where they were thatching.

As I went back the way I had come I suddenly realized that this detail had slipped me by until this moment when my mind and all my senses were operation in adrenalin-driven into overdrive. The houses were new and for the most part unfinished. At least half of them still lacked their full head-dress of thick dried elephant grass thatch and there was a constant movement of people around me and above me, working to complete the job of creating homes out of nothing more than what the scrubby grasslands might give. In the end there would be a kind of permanence in what they were doing, an island in the ocean of grass through which the cattle moved, the cattle they had lost. The well had tied them to this place. Now there was a crop here and there was water.

Of course, it had always been this way and I was not the first to see it and to think about it; there was nothing new in finding Jacob and Esau in an old landscape. And at the same time it could all be all undone in the twinkling of an eye. The houses took no more than a few days to build and they would be abandoned when the dictates of food aid and security and the thin mask they gave to political control intervened to move all these people up to Boma. Nothing was very permanent out here in the rangelands and the toic, not even the hold a man might have on reality or perhaps even on things more precious still.

I could feel myself calming down as I retraced my steps without too much difficulty. The walking and the thinking helped. I stopped to get a grip on where I had got to and realized that behind the next house I could see the tops of the acacia trees beyond the well where the Landcruiser was parked. The path bent sharply to the left around the round side of a hut and with my next few steps I found myself thrust out into the open space between the villages and the well. Over in the west, towards the small hillside where the elders had been reclining the previous afternoon, I could see a small crowd of women and men, near naked and dusty. Some of the men had decorated their hair with red mud and it glowed a deep throbbing terracotta red in the sunlight, like the African earth itself.

As I got closer, I saw that the crowd was gathered around my colleagues, who were seated on large stones each with a pile of papers on his lap. Simon was talking in Murle and a young man in shorts, probably the same one who had accompanied him the previous evening, was translating his words into Jiye. At the end of each delivery there was a pause, into which the twittering of the weaver birds in the acacia trees and the scarcely perceptible murmur of the slight breeze that had begun to stir the parched grasslands flowed and merged into the great silence that would have prevailed so easily over all of this world.

It was something I always noticed at these meetings. There was never an immediate surge of voices jostling one another, clamouring to be heard. Every look and every line on every face was wrinkled and puckered into a scowl of deep concentration, as though new concepts were being formed through a birth process that was painful and needed effort and time. Two worlds had met and were still finding out that the languages they spoke had grown up out entirely different sets of images and ways of connecting them into thoughts and concepts and so distilling this into words and meaning. And when they spoke, their voices were soft, hesitant and unsure. They did not interrupt one another and the words that came were slow.

I spoke the word of greeting, sat down on the ground next to John and Simon and surveyed the group of people before me. The old men were sitting on top of empty sacks, cut open and spread like towels in the dust. They sat with their feet together close in front of their naked groins and with the long shins spread upwards in a widening v shape, allowing them to rest their elbows on their knees. Every part of their physique was long and thin. The women sat with their legs stretched out in front of them and the naked children stood around and watched in deep, absorbed silence.

Simon looked up and smiled from below the baseball cap that shaded his eyes from the growing glare. The he spoke. 'Here you are, Richards. What kept you so long? It seems we are doing all the work to fill in your precious forms for you today!'

I smiled back and nodded. I did not feel any kind of reaction inside to the undisguised challenge in Simon's words and in his voice and smile. Rather I was aware, with an immediacy that was disconcerting in its clarity, of how disengaged I was feeling inside from everything now. The forms were not my forms at all and I was glad that the others were doing this task, leaving my mind to drift, disengaged, through the sea of images that imposed themselves on it like an endless series of photographs. I noticed that Simon was wearing a t-shirt with the strangely androgynous features of Michael Jackson's face spread, larger than life, across it, covering his chest. Normally he wore nothing particularly noticeable, a shirt hanging outside his trousers like the rest of them. The t-shirt was incongruous, the famous face had a curious expression that might have been a smile, but equally might have been a leer or a curse. It seemed to depend on how the person wearing the t-shirt moved or the expansion and contraction of his chest each time he breathed.

'I lost my way. I tried to find you in the village,' I said.

Simon laughed. It occurred to me that he always laughed, because underneath it all he was nervous really. The snigger – because that was what it was, not a real heartfelt laugh - was just a barrier that he put up. Everyone had their own barriers and his was this stupid laugh that could be so irritating in the intense heat, but which really did not signify anything at all. I pulled my Tilley hat off and used it to wipe the sweat from my brow.

John smiled gently in my direction. 'We are talking about what they eat,' he said.

I noticed a small pile of round tubers, like rough, shriveled potatoes, that had been piled on the ground at the feet of one of the old women. Next to it there were a few long, green leaves like one of the ingredients of an Italian salad.

'That it?'

'Yes, my friend,' said Simon, 'that is what they have to eat, that is all.' His voice carried an arrogant, angry undertone now, as though he wanted to blame me in some way for the people's destitution.

'They have the maize, too, and it is ready now in the field,' added John, 'but without their cows normal life is difficult for them.'

I looked across at the people of the village, sitting patiently under the unshaded sun that was climbing towards its zenith and staring at me. I sensed that they were waiting.
'What did you tell them?' I asked, turning to Simon. 'Did you tell them about the food aid at Boma.'

'No,' said Simon.

'Why not?'

'There is nothing to tell.' Again the arrogant look infused his features and this time he did not smile.

'But I thought you said you were going to include them in the distribution at Boma? You said they would have to move there for that and for their security, too.'

'I cannot say these things today,' said Simon. 'I must talk to Rumbek on the radio. And you must put all these things you see into your report so that WFP can put some extra food in the next drop. Then we will move them. Until then there is nothing we can do.'

'But you can see these people need help. They are poorer than all the others we have seen so far. They have nothing, they have lost their livelihoods. Look at the children, look at their arms and legs. They look like matchsticks.'

'Richards, my friend,' said Simon, smiling again with a leer that matched the ambiguous over-friendly malice of the t-shirt figure across his chest, 'You sound like Father Severino! Have you fallen in love with these people, too?'

'I'm doing my job.' I felt a momentary tensing of the muscles in my arms and upper body as I spoke, the brittle feeling that comes a split second before you commit yourself to a fight. But I could hear my voice sounding tired and weak and I knew I simply did not have the energy to drive this half-hearted stirring of anger and indignation inside beyond s slight melting of the artifice of detachment I had been self-indulgently building. It was hot, of course, and I needed a drink. Besides, I had not slept. My brain was not sharp or focused. The sentences stayed short and often repeated themselves. I felt the dryness of my palate with my tongue and then heard words flow out between my lips, as though another person was speaking them while I sat and watched. I wished I could get a drink and lie down to sleep.

'This could become a real emergency,' the voice was saying. 'The children will die.'

'When we get back to Boma we can tell Loki on the radio,' said John. 'Maybe then can include some additional resources in the drop that Daniel has come to prepare.'

'Yes,' said Simon. 'Or perhaps the leader can use his Thuraya?' He said this almost lightly, as though making a joke. But then he added in a sharper voice. 'It will still require the agreement of the SRRC.'

This easy lurching back into the bureaucracy that had been created to ensure the power of Simon and his ilk was like a new and sharper goad. I knew that real strength always lay in silence, but I was not strong in any case. 'Of course,' I said, standing up. 'It always needs that, doesn't it?' I could feel the anger coming now, good and hot inside. I had recaptured the voice and it was mine again. 'You and your friends in the SPLA!,' it snarled. 'You don't care for anybody, really. You're just playing games to build up your power base. You terrorise the people wherever you are and everyone is living in fear underneath it all. Nobody can go anywhere without your say-so. They need a permit just to move from one village to another. Maybe by the time you've decided to issue permits for all these people here they'll be dead.'

Simon said nothing. He remained seated, still smiling. The slight upward curl of his lip was a challenge, just as sure as if he had thrown down a leather gauntlet. It invited me to cross the line that held together the whole massive, surreal operation with all its crazy, complex net of rules and procedures and guidelines.

I could see the apprehensive look in John's eye, as I stood there facing Simon, but something else was driving me now to say my lines until the speech was complete with every detailed syllable of a text which it seemed I had crafted long before and had been carrying in my mind like a wriggling, irritating parasite waiting to burst out through his skin. 'You torture people, don't you?' I said. 'My office deals with the humanitarian principles cases, you know, so I know everything. There was that Sudanese who came from Australia to work for an NGO last year. Remember what happened to him? The SPLA said he was a spy. They tied him up with wire and beat him to a pulp. I saw the pictures.'

Simon stood up. The smile had left his face. 'When I speak to Rumbek,' he said, 'you will be PNG'ed and you will never enter the New Sudan again. So stay here with your friends until it is time to go. You will never come back!'

He turned and spoke briskly to the young men and then walked away with them across the open space towards the well and the vehicles beyond.

'He will cool down,' said John slowly. 'But you should have not said those things. You should not provoke these people.'

'He really pissed me off, John!'

'We have to work with him.'

'Maybe you do and maybe Father Severino does, but I'm going to be PNG'ed and I'm going to lose my job anyway, so I don't,' I could feel the rage that had been bottled up for so long blinding me and boiling my brain the way it had every time I found myself trekking out under the unforgiving sun because nobody else cared enough to get up early. In that moment I wanted to curse the whole lot of them to hell, including the priest. Then I caught the calm gaze of the other man. He looked concerned. He must be seeing something pretty bad. I sucked in air and closed my eyes, exhaling the tension in long, steady breaths. 'I should not be making trouble for you,' I said 'I'm sorry.'

'Don't worry,' said John. 'I know Simon well. There is no problem for me!'

I looked up into his face. Most of the people of the grasslands were taller and larger than I was and so I was always looking upwards into their faces. The thought came to me that I had never seen John's face marred by anger. 'There was always a gentleness and a kindness in his eyes and in the broad mouth. I smiled, not from the inside, but as a deliberate conciliatory gesture . 'I know you're right. I'm just tired.'

I looked up and saw the villagers were leaving quietly, heading back towards their homes.

'We got some data, anyway' said John. 'We can put it in the report.'

'Did you use your beans?'

'No, not today. There was no time in the end!'

We set off in Simon's footsteps.

It was time to go, it was two o'clock in the afternoon and the sun was beating down out of a sky without clouds, blue and throbbing. The rays came down and found us in the feeble shade under the acacias where we were packing the equipment into the back of
the Landcruiser and there was no escape. My arms and neck were burnt. The sweat dripped down from my scalp under the rim of my Tilley hat. It had been white a few days earlier when we set off from Loki. Now it was the same colour as the

earth under my feet, a mixed biscuit brown-brick red hue that seeped into everything, every item of clothing, every pore of skin, with the growing length of days lived in it and with it, sitting, sleeping and eating in this same dusty earth.

Nobody said anything. They all had things to do. The Sudanese were dealing with the tents; Father Severino and Sister Lucy were putting the boxes equipments and the simple furniture away in the back of the vehicle. I made myself busy with my own gear, making sure that everything was in its right place in the rucksack. I did not really care about it. It seemed to belong somewhere in the past now, along with all the other things that had been important. Today we would all pile in and drive back up to Boma. Tomorrow the plane would come, or maybe the day after tomorrow. Then I would be gone and this would be all something in the past.

I was avoiding Simon. There was nothing more to be said between us, nothing that wouldn't be an affront to the dignity of one or the other. The confrontation had been building up, anyway. I had been almost wanting it, or at least feeling the pull of its inevitability, from the very start and in some way had known which way things would go, just as I knew my place was not here in Sudan. It could never be my place the way it was for Simon, or for John or Samuel, come to that, and even, as I had been able to see right from the moment of our first meeting, for Father Severino.

I was avoiding him too. I did not admit it to myself at first, but, hunched down over my rucksack, I knew for sure that I did not want to turn round and rise to my feet to be greeted by anyone and that included the priest. The idea of us speaking to each other was an awkward, uncomfortable one, like the meeting of two old friends who have become strangers with nothing much in common or to say to one another after a lot of time has flowed down different river beds.

Of course it all started with the realization that I had missed the dream, but then that had been in line with expectations, hadn't it? There was a kind of elemental enthusiasm, nothing more, which did not come in sharable doses. It belonged to one person and one person's vision's only, whatever you might think. And in the end it would turn out to be as compromised as everything else.

Now there was nowhere left to go except to climb into the back seat alongside my hot, sweaty colleagues and doze a little and sleep what I could on the bumpy track back up to the camp. Four hours or so of tough road.

No-one was there from the village to see us off. The place was silent in the heat. Father Severino climbed in last, turned on the ignition, crossed himself, made sure the vents for the air-conditioning were open and then shifted into gear and drove in a large careful circle round to where the track started.

# 11.

*Monday night and beyond*
I slipped gratefully into a half-waking, half-sleeping state almost as soon as the vehicle began to move. The air-conditioning was not working well and only a trickling flow of chilled air leaked lazily through to the back seat from the ventilator nozzles on the dashboard, hardly refreshing the stifling, unmoving atmosphere. My head felt heavy with the lack of sleep and the sun's assault. Along the seat John and Simon had their heads back against the headrests with their eyes closed. Directly in front of me Sister Lucy's head was slumped forward onto her chest. I closed my eyes and pressed the back of my head into the sweaty imitation leather of the headrest.

I needed to sleep. It seemed improbable now that I had spent the whole night out under the stars, leaning back against the vehicle and gazing up in a drift of unordered thoughts none of which had resolved itself into anything worth preserving into the dawn of the day. It was just the usual merry-go-round that took me nowhere, the endlessly repeated collapsing of image into doubt, like a reversal process through which experience might be converted into concepts and ideas, rationalized into a plan for living, if not for action. The lack of resolution had eroded time so that two, three or four hours might pass in the same space as five minutes. It was always the same loop. I wanted to shut it off now and shut out the chain of images, the small children, smiling, naked, spindly arms and legs glued onto round, swollen bellies, the women clustered round Father Severino, as though to reach out and touch his garments and somehow through that contact find release from whatever it was that brought them to him, the group sitting on the ground under the sun, smoking their gourd-pipes, and waiting in turn to answer the questions from the list.

Who was I now? There was no telling – at least, soon that would be the case. My contract would end in ten days' time. When I got onto the plane it would be to say goodbye forever to the endless landscapes of grass and doubt. But who was this 'I'? What was he going to become? I waited for sleep to come so as to put this question aside for the time being. There was comfort to be had in sleep. Children slept.

There were cabbages in the garden in Ethiopia and the garden gate had a funny little half-broken latch on it that you had to close behind you to make sure the giant tortoises did not get in to eat the cabbages.

A sudden jolt as the vehicle stopped brought me back into full consciousness. My head swung forward awkwardly and then banged against the headrest. I opened my eyes. 'What is it?'

'Puncture,' said Father Severino. He had already opened his door and was looking back at the rear wheel on his side.

We all climbed out slowly, clumsy with the heat. Daniel and the guard were the first to scramble up onto the roof in order to untie the spare wheel. They lowered it down to John and Samuel while Father Severino fished the big cruciform wheel spanner out from under the boxes at the back and started to loosen off the nuts before fitting the jack.

It was one of those awkward Toyota jacks that needed to be placed on top of a solid plank of wood to stop it from digging itself into the ground. Father Severino was already down on his back under the wheel trying to fit it under the rear axle, which left me with a rare opportunity to make myself useful. I went to the back of the vehicle and looked under the boxes for the sort of thing that was needed. I found it quickly enough, along with the cranking handle for the jack, and brought them back to the priest.

'Well, done, Richards,' said Father Severino, smiling at him through the dust that clogged the sweaty pores of his face. In spite of myself I felt a small warm feeling reaching into my chest, nothing much, but enough to make me pull back the corner of my lips in a return grimace. At the same, more than before, I felt resentful of the ease of this manipulation, resentful, however, not so much of anything the priest might have achieved, but of my own susceptibility, which was in the end little different from the instinctive conduct of a dog that has been beaten time and time again. There was nothing good or human in that warmth when you worked it out.

I shoved the wooden board underneath the jack and then fitted the heavy metal rod into the hole on its side. Father Severino got up and started cranking, but I stopped him. I reached forward and took the rod from his hands. 'You must be tired from driving, Father. Let me do a bit of work.'

The priest did not resist. He passed the jack handle to me and turned to help the other men. They had got the heavy wheel down onto the ground and were rolling it over towards the back of the vehicle. I went on cranking, bending down to check the jack was secure as the wheel rose up off the ground. Once it was well clear Father Severino undid the nuts fully and piled them neatly where they would not get lost. Then the men got down and lifted the wheel with the punctured tire off the hub.

'Usually I would have to do this alone,' said Father Severino. 'Like this it is easy.'

I jacked the axle up higher to allow enough clearance for the new, fully inflated tire. Five minutes later the entire job was done and John was giving each nut a final hard tweak with the spanner. Daniel handed round the cigarettes.

I took one and lit it with Daniel's lighter. As I smoked I looked around at the landscape. The previous day I had not really taken in how dry it all was down here away from the base of the hills where Boma lay. The ground was more bare earth, rock and dust than anything. The grass was sparse, silver tufts here and there between the acacias, which themselves were just a tangle of black twigs. Simon and his guard had climbed up onto the roof of the Landcruiser and were looking around on all sides, talking to one another in Murle. Father Severino and Sister Lucy went over to join them, standing by the side of the vehicle.

Simon laughed and then smiled down at us. 'We are on the wrong road, my friend,' he said. His dark glasses made it impossible to see who he was calling his friend.

'I must have been dozing at the wheel,' said Father Severino, 'and I guess I missed the turning.'

'So where are we heading?' I asked.

'This way is north,' said Simon. He laughed again, harshly this time. 'If we go far enough we will come to the GOS enclave at Pibor Camp and you can go and stay with your friends from Khartoum!'

'But it's a long way to there… There is no real risk?…'

'Don't worry; we can correct this mistake easily. We will turn round and retrace our tracks until we find the right way.'

'Just as long as we have enough fuel,' said Father Severino. 'I did not bring any spare jerry cans.'

'We'll be ok,' said Simon. 'Once we are on the right road, if we run out of fuel we can walk the rest of the way. For us Sudanese it is nothing at all. You foreigners can sit and wait till we come back with fuel. It will not be a problem.'

The habitual mockery in his voice had hardened into a more serious tone in which pride and scorn coexisted together with something else that was more troubling, a bitter, volatile element made up of national or racial identity and a pride that merged into scorn as he drawled the word 'foreigners' at the same time as looking over towards us through his dark glasses. The foreigner might be richer beyond anyone's dreams, flying in planes, bringing endless deliveries of grain and other goods as though they were nothing, but here, right out here under a sun that did not relent and did not forgive mistakes, lost among the whispering silver grasslands, none of that counted for anything. Those who belonged here would survive with or without what the foreigners brought.

Everyone got back into the Landcruiser and Father Severino swung it around in a gentle circle, avoiding large stones, back onto the track pointing back the way we had come. 'I don't know how I could have made that mistake,' he said, more to himself than truly out loud. He was concentrating hard on the road ahead, swerving occasionally to keep out of the deepest ruts left by some heavy lorry possibly years previously.

After about half an hour Simon conferred briefly with the guard and then pointed to a faint track splitting off to the left. 'That's a short cut,' he said. 'Take it, Father. It will bring us back onto the right road.'

Father Severino slowed right down, looking doubtful. The track was no more than a cattle trail through the rough bush.

'Come on, Father,' said Simon, smiling. 'Trust me. I know my way out here.' The dark glasses hid his eyes. There was just the movement of the lips. He sat back, stretching his back up against the car seat like a cat. 'It is a short road.'

Father Severino said nothing as he eased the heavy vehicle onto the narrow track. The grass that surrounded and covered the track became taller almost immediately and he was forced to peer forward through the windscreen looking for hidden boulders.

We drove on for something like an hour. Our slow pace through the unchanging landscape in the heat made a mockery of any sense of time passing and the whole afternoon seemed to away in the space of less than ten kilometres. I had said I had no strong desire to arrive at our destination and by that I had meant that I could see no future beyond their arrival other than my own departure for ever from this land and from this life. It seemed logical enough not to be in hurry to embrace this change, unlooked-for and threatening. Yet, even so, I found the crawling pace irritating. My eye traveled backwards and forwards across the road ahead, towards the horizon and back, restless, searching for change.

Then, as though I had willed it, the change was upon us. The ground sloped abruptly away below into the stony bed of a dried-up river some twenty metres down. It stretched in both directions, a gash right across the landscape, worn down like a canyon by the flash floods of uncounted rainy seasons.

Father Severino brought the vehicle up to the brink, put the clutch in and shifted across to the low ratio gearbox.

'Easy!' said John, leaning forward from his position in the middle of the back seat.

The vehicle lurched forward over the edge and almost at once began to slide on the loose gravel. Father Severino dabbed the brakes with no effect on the accelerating progress of the heavy vehicle down the slope. Then he pushed the pedal down fully, holding it down, getting no response and then pumping it desperately, while he struggled to steer. We were swerving violently now as the heavy vehicle gathered even greater speed.

I heard someone shout from the back 'What's going on?' and Father Severino's frantic response 'The brakes aren't working.' Then Sister Lucy shrieked and there was a bang, incredibly loud right inside my ear, it seemed, as the world turned over suddenly and light and blackness changed places like a light switched rapidly off and on several times.

I was sitting on the ground, cross-legged. I did not know how or why I had emerged into the world in this position. I raised my eyes and saw some twenty yards ahead of me there was an upside down vehicle. Beneath me the ground was made up of small pebbles. A large black ant walked across the space between my knees. I wondered if there could be more of them coming towards me. They would bite. I should probably move. I reached forward to change position and was met with a sudden stab of pain in the area of my right collar bone. Every other part of my body ached, too.

I sat back for a moment and the missing time began to flow back into my conscious mind. We had been travelling along an unknown small trail. There had been a river bed to cross and we had started to go down. That was when the memory became more difficult – confused and incomplete, mainly just images, like stills replacing movie footage for a few frames. There had been the shrill note of Sister Lucy's call of alarm just as we started to spin.

John came up. 'Are you alright, Richards?' he asked.

'I think so, just a pain in my shoulder, or more like my collar bone. What about you?'

'I am fine. So is everybody else, thanks be to God. Except Father Severino. He is hurt.'

Samuel came round from behind him. 'He has hurt his collar bone,' said John, addressing him with a gesture towards me.

'Hello Richards, you are well, praise God!' said Samuel. 'Let me see your arm. Give it to me. Stretch it out front. Now try to raise it. Try!'

I could not move my straightened arm upwards beyond the horizontal. 'You have broken your clavicle,' said Samuel. 'Your collar bone,' he added. 'We'll just make a sling and then you'll be alright for now.'

The two men helped me to my feet and led me to the overturned vehicle, from which the box full of medical supplies had already been salvaged and opened. They pulled out a triangular bandage and quickly used it to make a sling for my arm.

It was like the first aid training from the security and survival course I had done when I first visited Loki. I had enjoyed doing it. It had made me feel like I was joining an elite team, special and newly inducted into the skills that would be required out here in the big empty land where they dropped you alone with your tent and your radio and your little pack of survival gear, including the Guinea Worm filter from the Carter Foundation and the condom which they told you could carry several litres of water if you needed it to.

'Come and see Father Severino,' said John.

The priest was lying on a blanket which they had spread in the shade of an acacia tree. Sister Lucy was sitting at his side, talking to him and adjusting his clothes. I squatted down next to them and asked what had happened.

Father Severino smiled. 'Just my leg,' he said. 'I got it caught between the pedals as we went over and it's twisted. Nothing serious. I'm fine.'

'But he cannot walk,' said Sister Lucy.

'That is right,' said John.

They all seemed very relaxed about everything, except for Sister Lucy. She scowled briefly at me, as though the accident and Father Severino's injury were something I had caused. I ignored her and asked John where Simon and the others had gone. He told me they had gone to the top of the river bed, on the other side. 'They will come soon,' he said. 'Meanwhile we can make a fire while we wait for them. You sit down here and we'll do it.'

So I sat in the shade with Sister Lucy and Father Severino, while John and Samuel gathered a large pile of dry bush wood together.

'We will need it tonight,' said Samuel. 'To keep the lions away.'

'Lions? I thought they were all dead,'

'Who knows,' said Samuel. 'Probably, but there may be one left. Or at least a hyena!' He laughed.

We lit the fire and brewed up a cup of tea. Simon, Daniel and the guard joined us almost before we had started to drink.

'So you are injured,' said Simon, looking me over briefly. 'But not too badly. That is good. There is almost no water, just a jerry-can a quarter full. We will leave it here for the ones who stay, but they will just be the weak ones. There will not be enough water for more. The rest of us will walk from here to Boma. It is not far and we will reach tonight. Then we can radio for the plane to come tomorrow to rescue you.' He looked at me. 'You will stay here, Richards, with the Father and Sister Lucy. The rest of us will walk fast.'

'Even Daniel?'

'Of course, why do you ask?'

'He is not Sudanese. He's a Kenyan. He walks no better than I do.' I could keep myself from sounding indignant, but it came out as something ridiculous in this wild place, a foolish little squawk of injured self-esteem.

'He has been in the field for many years,' said Simon firmly. 'He will be fine with us. But it is better for you to stay.'

I would have found some reconciliation to the way things were and had to be if he had added something then, some words to establish that I had been chosen to look after the injured priest and the nun. But he did not and his words hung in the air as he spoke them with all their loaded implication that I was simply not strong enough to take part in what the Sudanese could do and were willing to trust the Kenyan to do also. It felt as though he had won a final victory over me and had no need to grind my corpse any further into the dirt.

Later, after he and his followers had left, I came to wonder whether there was not something else motivating the decision as to who should go and who should stay. Maybe he had seen me in the maize field the night before with Sister Lucy. Nobody left out here would last long once the water was gone. And if men with guns came nobody would see or hear anything. They would just be gone. Whichever way I looked at it my time in command of anything, however, small, was over.

Everyone drank some tea. Daniel smoked and I smoked with him. When Simon had finished he put down his mug and stood up.

'We must go now,' he said. 'The plane will come to Boma tomorrow and we will come to fetch you.'

'If enough men can turn the car over, it will run again,' said Father Severino. The engine is not damaged.'

'We will bring a stretcher for you, Father Severino,' said Simon in reply.

I had my rucksack on the ground by my feet with all my travelling tools and toys inside it. I asked if they wanted my compass.

'No need,' said Simon. We know the way. This is our land. And this track will bring us to Boma, anyway.'

He filled his mug with water from the jerry can and drank it down. The ones who were going with him all did the same. Then they set off, walking fast.

I watched as they reached the top of the slope and then disappeared from view over the edge. Then I turned to Father Severino and Sister Lucy.

'I'll see what's in my pack,' I said. 'I have my toys. Some of them might be useful.'

The others said nothing. Sister Lucy was busy arranging the blanket on which Father Severino was lying, so that he could sit comfortably against the pile of boxes they had pulled out of the overturned vehicle. Rummaging with my one good hand I managed to dig out my torch, together with the flare and the emergency blanket. 'This is going to be useful, if they look for us with the plane,' I said. 'If you spread it out it reflects the sun like a big mirror.'

Neither of the other two said anything and I realized I was talking out loud to myself. Father Severino and Sister Lucy had their rosaries out and were performing their devotions together in low voices. I repacked my things in silence.

The hours went by gently in a silence that seemed to be natural or in some way required, like the silence inside a church. The heat of the day hardly diminished but the searing blast of the sun's direct rays relaxed as it sunk into the west and the shadows lengthened. Sister Lucy had dug out more blankets and I had placed my own on the far side of the fire from where we were sitting. 'There is nothing to eat,' she said, addressing both Father Severino and myself.

The priest said nothing in reply to this. For myself, I found I did not mind this news at all. I did not feel hungry, but already regretted not having asked Daniel to leave me at least two more of his cigarettes before he left. I wondered where they would have got to by now. Probably at least halfway to Boma and well in sight of familiar landmarks. Back in the narrow world whose twin axes were the SRRC compound and the airstrip.

I tended the fire. I gathered fuel of every kind and size from under the trees, small twigs as well as more substantial branches and one larger trunk. My injured collar bone hampered me in this task, since it meant I had to do everything with only one arm, but I was glad to have an activity with which to occupy myself. I did not want to sit around letting the thoughts that would chain themselves together flow into my mind. They were very close, I knew, circling like the wild animals of the African night. They would come and find me at night, but I would keep them away.

I realized that I had no idea of what animals there might be out there in the darkness. I had always assumed that, apart from the seasonal migrations of the white tailed cob across the border in this area, all the large stuff on four legs had been gunned down years before. The landscape was big and empty except for the wandering cattle and the people who followed the herds. But that did not mean there might not be some predators still out there, lurking in a hidden corner. They would come out at night to look for food, staying away from villages and cattle camps. If they had survived at all, it meant they would have learnt to hide themselves from the AK47s. They would patrol the darkness far from men and they might come to a place like this. A hyena might live in a place like this. The cover was good enough. Ethiopia had always been full of tales of hyenas breaking into lonely huts to steal children or killing drunkards as they staggered home to late at night.

I decided to keep the fire good and big and also to keep some long, strong sticks next to me. If I had to scare something away, I would be able to light the end of one and brandish it like a flaming a spear.

The sun dipped away below the rim of the river bed and the shadows became one.

I went round to the back of the vehicle to get the torch out of my pack. I found it quickly in one of the side pockets, switched it on to test the battery and then stuffed it into the long lower pocket of my bush trousers.

From out the darkness I could hear the voice of Father Severino calling out to me: 'Richards! Come and join us!' The tone was calm and full of that disconcerting inner warmth that had struck him the first time they had met. It was a tone that made you feel he really did want you to come over and join in whatever he was doing, like an offer of friendship that had neither been sought nor deserved. It was the very point of dusk now, the loneliest time of day, the time when, if ever, I could really do with a cigarette, and it felt as though the priest was calling me over at this precise moment out of some intuitive understanding of the workings of my inner self.

As I emerged from the darkness behind the vehicle, Sister Lucy shouted for me to bring some water. I tried pouring from the jerry can one-armed into a mug, but found I could not do it without a big risk of spilling the little water we had. I had no alternative but to take the jerry can over to her. She took it from me without speaking, looking straight and hard into my eyes. The severe lines of her big, dark face took on an additional harshness in the firelight that emphasized the thick black frame of her glasses. Then she spoke: 'You were there last night. I saw you.' Her voice was soft and smooth-toned. Like that it would not carry any distance beyond where we stood facing each other. It would not get anywhere near to earshot range for Father Severino.

That was all she said. I could sense anger in the way she turned away from me without saying anything further or making some token gesture of thanks for my help with the jerry can. I knew I could just let it go at this point, leaving everything else unsaid and only understood between us, but there was a bug inside me that was twitching and irritating my skin as it tried to force its way out. I stepped round to confront her face to face once more and grabbed the jerry can handle to stop her from leaving.

'I know you were there with Simon,' I said. 'I heard some of what you said. Do you understand? I know what is going on. I don't condone it, but it hardly comes as a surprise. Nothing comes for free out here, not even the right to do good. But there was a third person there with you, wasn't there. Another man. Who was it? Was it Daniel? That would make sense, wouldn't it? Someone with access to the planes. I could't work out why he had to turn up in Boma and why he came here with us.'

She looked at me for a moment with an intense concentration of energy, as though she was wondering whether to try to wrench the jerry can out of my one-handed grasp. 'What do you want?' she hissed. 'I have nothing more to say to you.'

'You don't like me,' I said. 'You didn't like me since the first time we met. I know why it is too. It's because I don't play the game the way we are supposed to, I don't go along with it. I see things as they are. I see Simon for what he is and I see John and Samuel. I see you, too, Sister. You have things the way you want them here and that is all you care about…'

'All I care about?' she echoed my words. 'Who are you to say such arrogant things? You have no idea at all. And you have no compassion. What I care about is him.' She nodded in the direction of Father Severino. 'Everything he does is good and pure. In all of this filth that you see and that you fill your mind with, he is the one holy man, the one servant of God, the only one who really loves God's children when everyone else has forgotten them or just wants to trample on them.'

I looked at her. The fierce anger in her eyes was not a lie. Her eyes told what her words would not. Whatever deals she was doing with Simon, whatever corruption she was prepared to let into her Garden of Eden, according to her logic her reason for doing it was in its own way compelling and pure. I followed the direction of her gaze over to where the priest was sitting, propped against the wrecked vehicle. In the end there was no telling what might really have brought him all the way out here to do his good works. Watching him you could choose to believe it was the love of God that provoked the sacrifice that was no sacrifice, or you could look for something else. Everyone had a reason for coming to this big, empty place.

'Don't say anything to him,' said Sister Lucy, freeing the jerry can from my grasp with a sudden jerk, 'whatever you may think of me, or of him.'

Her eyes were still angry and defiant, but there was a softer tone in her voice as she said this. I released my hold and stood still where I was for a few moments, taking in the bitterness of her anger. She carried a burden that might be made unbearable by the thought that someone else knew about it. She would have to live with that as long as I existed. Not that I was going to do anything about it.

'What about Simon?' I asked.

'What about Simon?' She echoed my question, her voice once again sharp and angry.

'Does he know I saw you?'

'I don't know.'

She turned away from me quickly. Perhaps the same thought had crossed her mind too. Perhaps Simon did know and perhaps that made a difference to how we should feel about our situation. He had not left a single one of his men to guard us, which was a breach of safety rules that could not lightly be explained. You could say he had abandoned us, although if his intention had been to let nature take care of us, it was an uncertain strategy at best. The alternative was something darker. Someone might come to find us, but that did not have to mean they would be coming to rescue us.

Out of the shadows I heard Father Severino calling me to join him. I went slowly over to where he was and sat down on a flat stone.

I knew I wasn't going to tell him anything and this knowing made me feel strong, although this knowledge did not liberate me. It made me part of the dirtiness and the filth and it made me feel sick. I did not want to test the priest. It wasn't because of the nun, either. I just did not want to know anything else.

'It's very swollen and bruised,' said Sister Lucy in reply to my asking Father Severino about his foot. 'Some bone is broken but we will need an x-ray to see.'

'We're a long way from an x-ray machine.'

'The ICRC have one, when we get back to Loki.'

'Maybe he should go straight to Nairobi.'

'Maybe…'

'But does it hurt, Father?' I asked.

'I would be lying if I said that it did not hurt,' he said.

'I'm sorry.'

'What for? You did not do this?'

And yet I could not escape from a sense of guilt that I knew came from my failure to find the purity of spirit within myself that would have let me enter through the gate that Father Severino had led me to and had for a while held open for me. I felt like a child who has destroyed all the goodness of a holiday trip by misbehaving and who knows inside that his misbehaviour has had no motivation other than his own inner badness and an urge to assert himself through denial of all the good things that could have been shared. 'I should have brought the Thuraya,' I said. 'I don't know why I forgot.'

'Your radio?'

'No, the sat phone. It would have worked instead of the radio. It works better, in fact. Then we could have contacted Loki security. Everything would have been much better.'

'I don't think that is necessarily so,' said Father Severino. 'And besides, look at the reality. I am the one who missed the right road and I am the one who crashed the car.'

'It was an accident. The brakes failed.'

'I knew there were problems with the brakes.'

'But I thought we fixed them the day before yesterday?'

'We tried to fix them, tried our best. And that is all we could do. The brake fluid must have leaked somehow. I do not know. But anyway we tried. Isn't that what matters? We have to be practical here to survive in this place. Right now do you think we are doing alright?'

'So far perhaps we are.'

'And our friends will easily reach Boma, if they have not already. They can move fast. If they thought they needed to they would even come back now in the dark to look for us.'

'Do you think they should?'

'Are you worried about something?'

'I expect it's just stupid, but I was wondering if there might be some risk from hyenas or lions.'

'I don't think so somehow. There would be more danger from men, a cattle raiding party, for example, or militia. But we are far away from any likelihood of that. We are alone here in the dark.'

'I'm sure you are right, but when the night comes it is easy to imagine other things. It's that primitive fear of the dark that has always been there.'

'And it is not often that you are so alone or the night is so dark.'

'Is that what brings people to God, a childish fear of the dark?'

'Maybe it is.'

'I'll just check the fire.'

I raised myself back up from the ground. Even this was a clumsy action with only one hand to use in order to push myself up from my cross-legged position. I went over and put several thick branches onto the top of the fire, staying to watch for a few minutes to ensure the flames caught. I stared into the red heat. I did not feel comfortable with myself. But I did not feel comfortable with the priest any longer, either, and the way we were skirting around the issues was not helping. I had not thought it through, but I had imagined that my conduct must have been so transparent that Father Severino would have wanted to say something about it. Hadn't I hurt his feelings in some way or done damage to his belief in the project he had set for himself? Hadn't I somehow put in question the whole conceptual enterprise that underpinned whatever it was that drew this man to these people? Did I have so little impact?

When I had finished with the fire I went back over and sat down again with him.

'I'm sorry, Father. Perhaps I owe you an apology. The fact is that when we were in the village, I didn't share the thing you were feeling. I knew you wanted me to share in it somehow, but I could not. It's as if there is a hard, cold filter that comes down in front of my eyes and, whatever I see, I am kept apart from it and all the time there is a voice in my ear questioning everything I may be feeling: sympathy, sadness, outrage, compassion, - especially compassion. I cannot feel close to the people – to anyone, for that matter. And when I feel pushed into it I close up entirely. They were your people, Father. The village is your place, not mine. I would have to find my own.

'But I don't think I am going to find such a place for myself, Father, because all the time I have questions in my mind. I question everything. Everything we are doing. I see the dirty things that people do, too, the ones who say they are there to help and the ones being helped too, all of them. And I find I don't believe in any of it in the end. I can't get enthusiastic, I can't see the point, except that I'd feel even worse if I wasn't doing something.'

I paused for a moment, feeling the end of this rhetoric like an actor on stage coming to the end of his big speech. Then I added the final touch of melodrama: 'My career is coming to an end anyway. I knew that before I came on this mission.'

As I was speaking I knew inside that this was what I had meant to do over dinner on that first evening of our meeting. I had not been able to open the inner gate on that occasion, but now it seemed there was no stopping me. It must be due to the circumstances - the darkness, the firelight, the isolation of the place. I noticed that Sister Lucy had edged away towards the fire, where she had placed a kettle to boil. I did not feel any need for this tact on her part. I did not resent her presence at all. I felt I probably would not have minded who was listening. I was speaking my lines out and the faces of the audience were hidden behind the footlights anyway.

'I don't believe in any of it, Father,' I said. 'You listen to all the great gurus and people talking about development. They go and on about it, how it's going to pull everyone out of poverty through this thing called growth. And they boast about the number of people who have been pulled out of poverty, how big it is. And people believe them. They believe the big lies they tell. I know, because I did – when I was young and full of energy and enthusiasm. But in the end you see it is all futile. They lie, you see. When they talk about people being pulled out of poverty, they always talk about percentages, but the fact is that the population of the world is growing all the time, so the real, absolute number of people living shitty lives is bigger now than ever before, even if you stretch your imagination far enough to agree with the World Bank people and the U.N. people in their nice economists' suits that the filthy slums around all the big cities are somehow a step up from living poor in a remote mountain hut. Or down in the toic, if it comes to that. You know that is all that is waiting for this place? When the peace comes, they'll pour their money in and Juba or Rumbek or wherever they choose will just become an enormous shanty town, an endless slum of broken dreams.

'I worked out why it is, by the way. It's all because of a thing they call redundancy. It's how nature works. It's more true than the old thing about nature abhors vacuum. Nature loves too much. It's how languages work and how electric circuits work. Spare capacity. You get maximum efficiency if you have greater capacity than you need. If you have an exact match it breaks down. It's how economics works. You always need more people than you actually need. You need the ones at the bottom for the others to stand on. It's the big lie when they say growth will make everything good for everybody. It just doesn't work like that...'

I felt a sharp perception of my voice trailing off. I was listening to myself from a distance, not very interested.

*Blah blah blah! My voice drones on, but underneath it all there is no substance, just the three of us alone out here with the dirty little secret we share...*

Father Severino leaned forward slightly and in the dim, reddish light that came from the fire behind him I could see that there was sweat round the top of his face and that he was clenching his teeth.

'Your foot is hurting you, Father?' I asked.

'It is a little. It seems to have got worse now. But do not worry about that, Richards, I have one thing to say to you. Help me to sit properly.'

I got up and went around behind Father Severino. I would have liked to manhandle him into a more comfortable position, but I would have needed two arms for that, so I did my best adjusting the backrest of boxes.

'Listen, Richards,' said the priest, when I had finished. 'I do not feel able to talk a lot now. I am tired and the pain makes it difficult to think. You are a strange man. You do not even share the name your mother gave you. You hide it. Maybe you hide it from yourself, too. I don't know. I am tired. But remember what I said to you before. It is good that you ask questions, that you are honest with yourself. You must care about something or you would not ask questions. Maybe that is all you have for now.'

It did not seem like much of an answer and it left me with the same querulous challenge in my mind. 'Ok, Father,' I said. 'What about the village. What about that? Wasn't it supposed to be different?'

The priest looked at me intensely for a moment and then spoke quietly. 'I know what you mean,' he said. 'And maybe it's me who owes you an apology…' He did not say anything more, but just let his words hang in the silent darkness as his head drooped in obvious fatigue forward down towards his chest. And in fact there was nothing else to say. That was obvious, it seemed, to both of us.

Sister Lucy brought mugs of tea over and we drank in silence.

Then for no particular reason other than to break the silence I said 'Tomorrow we'll be out of here!'

'We may even see the plane fly over,' said Father Severino and for some reason the three of us all laughed.

'We should sleep,' said Sister Lucy. 'The Father is exhausted.'

I said goodnight to them. I built up the fire and then took out my torch in order to see inside my pack, holding it between my teeth while I rummaged. I found the small guide to the stars which I had always carried with me right from the beginning, from the times when I had been young and enthusiastic. I did not feel like sleeping and the sky above my head seemed brighter with stars than it had ever done before.

I made my way carefully up the side of the river bed, planting my footsteps in the small circle of light cast by the torch. If I could get up onto the plain the view of the stars would be unobstructed on all sides. I would sit with my book and do as I had always done, staring up for long enough to allow my eyes to grow accustomed to the darkness and then to make out the mystical shapes into which the stars were grouped, before switching on the torch and checking my observations with the charts in the book.

From the rim I looked back down at the glowing light of the fire with the shadowy forms of my two companions to one side, the overturned vehicle on the other. For a few moments I had a sensation of departure, as though I were saying goodbye forever to them and to everyone else I had been with. That would not be until I got onto the plane, of course, and even then some of them would be with me on the flight. But now the sensation of sudden, irredeemable rupture came hard upon me nonetheless. I spat to clear my mouth of the thick saliva that had built up during the brief climb. Then I turned and set off along the track.

It did not take long to find what I was looking for, a big flat stone which I could sit on or even lie back on without fear of scorpions or snakes. Over to the left was a small outcrop with a flat stone on top. I made my way slowly away from the track between sharp, thorny plants and loose stones, until I reached it and could sit down on top of its smooth surface. It was a large, flat slab, still radiating the warmth poured onto it throughout the day by the sun. It was a fine, sturdy rock, safe and warm, with an almost maternal feel. I lay back and gazed up at the stars above me. I did not need the book to trace the line of Orion's belt and out along it to Aldebaran and eventually the Pleiades. The stars were silver and the sky was a black velvet cloth behind them. I would be safe up here, hidden from view, but able to see.

I wondered if the woman and the child would come and find me here. Perhaps here I would hear their voices. I closed my eyes, waiting. But they did not come. They would only come when I was sleeping, I knew. It would be more probable that a tribal raiding party would come along, or a jeep full of militia, Dr. Melchior's men? If people came unexpected, would they kill everyone they found? Did they always do that? I did not know. It was all abstract speculation. I knew nothing. I had not even been near the scene of a home-made bomb being pushed out of the back of an Antonov. I knew nothing about this country and its scars. Part of me had been hoping there would be an incident, something cataclysmic, a violence that would catch me up in the sweep of history, however trivial and far away from the things that mattered to the rest of the world, but enough for me in my own little world, enough to keep the empty future at bay.

Now what I knew was that I was alone and I knew there was a façade that I had set up behind which I could hide and posture, but that now the façade was about to crumble. I had run out of places to hide myself in. I had not looked beyond this mission when I accepted it. It had been scheduled as my last before the termination of my contract and I had made no plans for a future beyond it. In a way I had meant it to be terminal. But I knew now that there was no end, there could never be. The voices did not go silent. There was no off switch, no easy way out. And I knew that I did not want to die alone, even though I suspected that that might be where I was heading. I did not want to be cut off from all humanity and warmth in the immensity of this solitude.

Maybe I would spend the night up here on this stone, or maybe go back down to join the priest and the nun by the fire. But part of me would go back down across the river bed and then up to the other side to disappear among the trees and prickly shrubs and grasses in the starlight, heading west into the bush.

*Manila, April 2008, revised June and December 2010, May and December 2011 and February 2012.*

# End note: abbreviations

'The Humanitarian' takes place in the setting of a long-standing civil war, complicated by factions, militias and splinter groups reflecting far older, deep-seated divisions, mostly along ethnic lines. Its theme is a humanitarian operation whose longevity, complexity and divisiveness had by the time in which the story is set come in many ways to mirror those divisions. One aspect of this complexity was a multiplicity of acronyms that to the outsider or the newcomer could often combine to form a wall of jargon as impenetrable as the swamps themselves, a kind of barrier to keep such interlopers out, or at least to overwhelm and humble them. I have done my best to eliminate the use of jargon from the text but inevitably have felt obliged to include it in appropriate places in order to try to recreate the atmosphere of that place and time. If the reader is at first bewildered or, better still, irritated by these unfriendly intrusions, then I hope he or she will at least take comfort in the authenticity of their experience.

The following is a partial list, which will, I hope, help make things clearer in the end.

OLS            Operation Lifeline Sudan
*(Name of the combined humanitarian operation in South Sudan)*

NGO            Non-governmental Organisation

*(jargonese for 'charity')*

(UN)OCHA            United Nations Office for the Coordination of Humanitarian Affairs
*(UN body providing staff for the UN emergency coordinator)*

WFP — World Food Programme
*(UN body responsible for delivering emergency food aid)*

SPLM — Sudan Peoples' Liberation Movement
*(Main rebel movement in South Sudan)*

SPLA — Sudan Peoples' Liberation Army
*(Its military wing)*

SRRA — Sudan Relief and Rehabilitation Association
*(Relief wing of the SPLM)*

SPDF — Sudan Peoples' Defense Force
*(Rebel Faction mainly representing the Nuer tribes)*

RASS — Relief Association of South Sudan
*(Its relief wing)*

SRRC — Sudan Relief and Rehabilitation Commission
*(Name given to the combined SRRA and RASS when they officially joined forces in 2002)*

Printed in Great Britain
by Amazon.co.uk, Ltd.,
Marston Gate.